GREECE TRAVEL GUIDE

*The Most Complete Full-Color Pocket Edition
Unearthing Greece's Hidden Treasures*

STEVAN CLARK

TABLE OF CONTENTS

Chapter 1 – Introduction
Greece: A Journey to the Cradle of Civilization

*A*ncient and modern, chaotic yet charming, Athens is a city of paradoxes that beckons travelers with its rich history, vibrant culture, and a lively food scene. The sprawling metropolis is a treasure trove of historic sites, fascinating museums, bustling markets, and inviting eateries, all waiting to be discovered. In this chapter, we embark on a virtual exploration of Athens, guiding you through its labyrinthine streets and shedding light on its intriguing character. We delve into an overview of the city, providing key insights that will set the stage for your Athenian adventure.

We journey back in time, visiting Athens' celebrated historic sites and museums, where relics of the past whisper tales of glory and grandeur. From the awe-inspiring Acropolis to the insightful National Archaeological Museum, we delve into the heart of Greece's historic and cultural heritage.

Food is central to the Greek way of life, and in Athens, the culinary scene is a delectable blend of tradition and innovation. We'll guide you through local cuisine and the array of dining options, from charming tavernas serving soulful homemade dishes to elegant restaurants offering modern twists on classic recipes.

Finally, we'll guide you through the vibrant shopping landscape of Athens, where local markets brim with artisanal crafts, and upscale stores showcase the best of Greek design.

Immerse yourself in this chapter to gain a well-rounded understanding of Athens and its abundant offerings, providing a solid foundation for your impending journey.

Why Choose Greece

Welcome to the enchanting world of Greece, where ancient legends come alive against a backdrop of stunning landscapes and crystal-clear waters. Choosing Greece as your travel destination promises an unforgettable adventure, blending history, culture, and natural beauty in perfect harmony. Let's explore the compelling reasons why Greece should be at the top of your travel bucket list.

A Tapestry of History and Culture: Greece is a land steeped in history and culture, boasting a legacy that has profoundly influenced the world. Delve into the wonders of ancient Greece, where philosophy, democracy, and the arts were born. Wander through ancient ruins, and let history whisper its tales as you stand before the awe-inspiring monuments of the past.

Idyllic Mediterranean Climate: Embrace Greece's Mediterranean climate, offering warm summers and mild winters. The sun-kissed beaches beckon you to relax and unwind, while the pleasant weather creates the perfect atmosphere for exploring both ancient sites and natural wonders.

Greek Hospitality and Traditions: Experience the warmth of Greek hospitality, where locals open their hearts and homes to visitors. Embrace age-old traditions, indulge in vibrant festivals, and savor mouthwatering cuisine that reflects the essence of the Mediterranean lifestyle.

Breathtaking Landscapes and Islands: Greece's landscapes are a symphony of diversity, from the rugged mountains of the mainland to the pristine beaches of its iconic islands. Each island has its unique charm, promising an array of experiences, from romantic sunsets over Santorini's caldera to vibrant nightlife on the streets of Mykonos.

A Mecca for Food Enthusiasts: For food lovers, Greece is a gastronomic paradise. Savor the flavors of fresh seafood, locally-sourced olive oil, tangy feta cheese, and sweet baklava. Immerse yourself in the lively culture of Greek tavernas, where dining becomes a celebration of life.

Adventure and Activities: Whether you're an adrenaline junkie or seeking serene nature escapes, Greece has it all. Hike through breathtaking trails, sail across the azure waters of the Aegean Sea, or explore underwater wonders through snorkeling and diving adventures.

Timeless Myths and Legends: Greece is the land of myths and legends, where tales of gods and heroes come alive. Stand on the grounds of Olympia, the birthplace of the Olympic Games, and feel the echoes of ancient competitions that continue to inspire the world.

Embarking on a journey to Greece means embarking on a transformative experience, where history intertwines with modernity and where the hospitality of its people leaves an indelible mark on your heart. In the following chapters, we'll guide you through the wonders of Greece, helping you craft memories that will linger long after you leave its shores. So, pack your bags and let's set sail for the cradle of civilization!

CHAPTER 2 - BEST TIME TO VISIT

*C*hoosing the best time to visit Greece depends on your preferences and the experiences you seek. Each season offers a distinct charm and a range of activities to enjoy. Let's explore the different seasons in Greece and what they have to offer:

- **Spring (March to May):** Spring is a delightful time to visit Greece, as the landscape awakens with blooming flowers and lush greenery. The temperatures are mild and pleasant, making it ideal for outdoor activities such as hiking and sightseeing. Spring is also the season for Easter celebrations, an important religious and cultural event in Greece.
- **Summer (June to August):** Summer is the peak tourist season when Greece shines in all its glory. The weather is hot and sunny, and the beaches are at their best. It's the perfect time to indulge in water sports, beach hopping, and island adventures. However, be prepared for larger crowds and higher prices, especially in popular tourist destinations.
- **Autumn (September to November):** Autumn brings a comfortable transition from the scorching summer, and the weather remains pleasant throughout September and October. It's an excellent time to explore historical sites and engage in outdoor activities without the summer crowds. The sea is still warm, making it enjoyable for swimming and snorkeling.
- **Winter (December to February):** Winter in Greece is milder compared to other European countries, but it can still be chilly and rainy. If you prefer a quieter experience and don't mind cooler temperatures, winter can be a magical time to visit. You can explore ancient sites without the crowds, enjoy winter sports in the mountain regions, and experience local traditions during Christmas and New Year's celebrations.
- **Shoulder Seasons:** The shoulder seasons, which fall between the peak and off-peak times, can be an excellent compromise for travelers seeking a balance between pleasant weather and fewer tourists. These periods include late spring (May to June) and early autumn (September to October).
- **Considerations for Island Hopping:** If your itinerary includes exploring multiple Greek islands, keep in mind that ferry schedules may be more limited during the off-peak months. In contrast, the summer months offer more frequent ferry connections between islands.
- *No matter which season you choose, Greece welcomes you with open arms and a plethora of experiences waiting to be discovered. Whether you're basking in the summer sun on a sandy beach, admiring ancient ruins against a vivid sunset, or savoring traditional Greek delicacies, every moment in Greece is a journey of wonder and delight. Plan your visit based on your preferences, and Greece will reward you with memories that will linger for a lifetime.*

CHAPTER 3 - HISTORY AND CULTURE

*G*reece's rich history and vibrant culture are at the heart of its allure as a travel destination. *From the birthplace of democracy to its profound influence on art, philosophy, and literature, Greece's historical significance is unparalleled. In this section, we will delve into the captivating history of Ancient Greece and its enduring influence on the world.*

ANCIENT GREECE AND ITS INFLUENCE

Ancient Greece holds a remarkable place in human history, leaving an indelible mark on Western civilization. Its influence can be felt in various aspects of modern life, including politics, philosophy, architecture, and the arts. Here are some key aspects of Ancient Greece and its enduring impact:

- **Birthplace of Democracy:** Ancient Greece is credited with establishing the world's first democratic system of government in the city-state of Athens around the 5th century BCE. Citizens were actively involved in decision-making, and this groundbreaking concept of democracy laid the foundation for many modern political systems.

- **Philosophy and Thinkers:** The great philosophers of Ancient Greece, such as Socrates, Plato, and Aristotle, have profoundly shaped the way we think and reason even today. Their teachings on ethics, metaphysics, and politics continue to be studied and admired across the globe.

- **Olympic Games:** The Olympic Games, first held in Olympia around 776 BCE, were a prominent sporting event in Ancient Greece. These games, held every four years, celebrated physical prowess and unity among city-states. The modern Olympic Games pay homage to this ancient tradition.

- **Architecture and Engineering:** Greek architecture is renowned for its elegance and harmony, with iconic structures like the Parthenon in Athens exemplifying classical design. Greek architects introduced innovative construction techniques, such as the use of columns and architraves, which continue to influence architecture worldwide.

- **Literature and Drama:** Ancient Greek literature produced timeless works, including epic poems like Homer's "Iliad" and "Odyssey." The Greeks also perfected the art of drama, with playwrights like Sophocles, Euripides, and Aeschylus creating enduring tragedies and comedies.

- **Art and Sculpture:** Greek art is characterized by its idealized depictions of the human form, reflecting the belief in the importance of beauty and balance. Marble statues like the "Venus de Milo" and the "Discus Thrower" are celebrated masterpieces from this era.
- **Legacy of Alexander the Great:** The conquests of Alexander the Great expanded the Greek influence across three continents, leading to the spread of Hellenistic culture. This cultural diffusion left a lasting impact on art, language, and customs in regions such as Egypt and the Middle East.

Visiting Greece allows travelers to immerse themselves in this extraordinary history, as remnants of ancient civilizations can be found throughout the country. Exploring archaeological sites like the Acropolis in Athens, the ancient theater of Epidaurus, and the Temple of Apollo in Delphi transports visitors back in time to a world of myth and greatness. Greece's ability to preserve and celebrate its historical heritage is a testament to the profound importance it places on its cultural legacy.

OVERVIEW OF GREEK MYTHOLOGY

Greek mythology, a captivating tapestry of gods, goddesses, heroes, and mythical creatures, is an integral part of Greece's cultural heritage. These timeless tales, once believed to be accounts of real events, have shaped art, literature, and philosophies for millennia. Understanding Greek mythology is key to comprehending the cultural nuances and symbolism found throughout the country. Here is an in-depth overview of the essential elements of Greek mythology:

The Gods and Goddesses: The ancient Greeks believed in a pantheon of gods and goddesses who governed various aspects of life. At the helm of this divine family was Zeus, the powerful god of the sky and thunder, who ruled over the other gods from Mount Olympus. Hera, Zeus's wife and sister, was the goddess of marriage and family. Other significant deities included Poseidon, god of the sea; Athena, goddess of wisdom and warfare; Apollo, god of the sun and arts; and Aphrodite, goddess of love and beauty.

The Myths and Legends: Greek mythology is replete with captivating myths and legends that explain the origins of the world, natural phenomena, and the lives of mortals. These stories often involve interactions between gods and humans, highlighting the complexities of human nature. Prominent myths include the creation of the world by the Titans, the epic adventures of Hercules (Heracles), the tragic love story of Eros (Cupid) and Psyche, and the heroics of Odysseus in the "Odyssey."

The Heroes: Greek mythology boasts an array of legendary heroes known for their courage, strength, and cunning intellect. Perseus, armed with the Gorgon's head, defeated the fearsome Medusa; Theseus slew the Minotaur in the labyrinth of Crete; and Achilles, known for his invulnerability, fought valiantly in the Trojan War. These heroic tales continue to inspire contemporary literature and art.

Mythical Creatures: Greek mythology introduced a plethora of mythical creatures that enchanted the imagination. The mighty Pegasus, a winged horse, became the companion of heroes in their quests. The Sphinx, with the body of a lion and the head of a woman, posed riddles to travelers. The fearsome Chimera, a hybrid creature, terrorized ancient lands. These fantastical beings add an element of wonder and awe to the stories of ancient Greece.

Symbolism and Influence: Greek mythology's influence permeates modern society. Its symbols are woven into literature, architecture, and even astronomy. The twelve signs of the zodiac have their origins in Greek mythology. For example, the constellation Orion was said to be a great hunter, and the Pleiades star cluster represents the seven daughters of the titan Atlas. By understanding these mythological references, travelers gain a deeper appreciation of Greek art and culture.

Religious Festivals: Ancient Greeks held religious festivals to honor and appease the gods. The most significant festival was the Panhellenic Olympic Games, dedicated to Zeus, which united city-states in friendly competition. Other festivals celebrated deities like Dionysus, god of wine and revelry, and Demeter, goddess of agriculture, through theatrical performances and processions.

Embracing Greek mythology while visiting Greece provides an enriching cultural experience. Exploring archaeological sites associated with mythical events, such as the Palace of Knossos in Crete, adds a sense of wonder to the journey. Additionally, attending local festivities and performances allows travelers to witness the enduring legacy of these ancient stories and the cultural reverence for their mythical heritage.

MODERN GREEK CULTURE AND TRADITIONS

While Greece is celebrated for its ancient past, its contemporary culture and traditions are equally captivating and deeply rooted in history. Modern Greek culture is a vibrant blend of ancient customs, religious practices, and regional diversity. Exploring the richness of modern Greek culture provides travelers with a profound understanding of the country's identity and its enduring connection to its past. Here are some key aspects of modern Greek culture and traditions:

Language and Communication: The Greek language, with its 3,000-year history, is an essential component of Greek culture. Although English is widely spoken in tourist areas, learning a few basic Greek phrases can enhance the travel experience and foster positive interactions with locals. Greeks take pride in their language, and efforts to communicate in Greek are often warmly received.

Religion and Orthodoxy: Religion plays a significant role in Greek culture, and the dominant faith is Greek Orthodoxy. Visitors to Greece will encounter numerous churches and monasteries, many of which are architectural masterpieces. Religious traditions are deeply ingrained in daily life, with regular church attendance and the celebration of religious holidays being integral to the culture.

Easter Celebrations: Easter is the most important religious festival in Greece, surpassing even Christmas in significance. The Holy Week leading up to Easter Sunday is marked by various rituals and customs, such as solemn processions, reenactments of Christ's Passion, and the lighting of candles at midnight during the Resurrection service.

Traditional Music and Dance: Music and dance are an inseparable part of Greek culture. Traditional music is often accompanied by instruments like the bouzouki, baglamas, and lyra. Folk dances, such as the syrtos and hasapiko, are performed during festivals, weddings, and other social gatherings, symbolizing unity and joy.

Greek Cuisine: Greek gastronomy is celebrated worldwide for its delectable flavors and healthy ingredients. Each region boasts its culinary specialties, with dishes often reflecting the abundance of local produce and seafood. Traditional Greek meals are an experience to savor, with shared dishes and an emphasis on community and togetherness.

Family and Social Life: Family is at the core of Greek society, and the concept of filotimo, or love of honor, emphasizes the importance of family bonds, hospitality, and respect. Gathering for meals with extended family and friends is a cherished tradition that reinforces social connections.

Name Days: In addition to birthdays, Greeks also celebrate name days, which are associated with the feast days of Orthodox saints. Name days hold a special place in Greek culture, and they are commemorated with well-wishes, gatherings, and small gifts.

Kefi and Philoxenia: Kefi is an untranslatable Greek word that encompasses the joy of living in the moment and celebrating life. Philoxenia, on the other hand, refers to the deep-rooted tradition of hospitality towards guests. Greeks are known for their warm and welcoming nature, making visitors feel like cherished friends.

Contemporary Arts and Literature: Greece has a rich artistic heritage that extends beyond its ancient history. Modern Greek artists, writers, and musicians continue to contribute to the cultural landscape. Exploring contemporary art galleries and attending literary festivals can offer insight into the country's evolving creative expression.

By engaging with modern Greek culture and traditions, travelers gain a more profound appreciation for the depth of the Greek experience. Embracing the warmth of Greek hospitality, savoring the flavors of local cuisine, and participating in age-old customs all contribute to an unforgettable journey into the heart of Greece's vibrant and enduring culture.

CHAPTER 4 - TRAVEL ESSENTIALS

Stepping into a journey requires meticulous planning and a thorough understanding of certain fundamental aspects, irrespective of the destination. In this chapter, we delve into some of the most essential elements that one needs to consider before embarking on their travels. From necessary documentation such as passport and visa requirements, to understanding health and safety guidelines, we aim to cover it all.

PASSPORT AND VISA REQUIREMENTS

Before embarking on a journey to Greece, it's crucial to ensure that all necessary travel documents are in order. Here is a comprehensive overview of passport and visa requirements for visiting Greece:

Passport Requirements:

All foreign visitors to Greece must possess a valid passport that remains valid for at least six months beyond their intended stay in the country. It is advisable to renew passports well ahead of their expiration date to avoid any travel disruptions.

Visa Requirements:

Greece is a member of the European Union (EU) and the Schengen Area. As such, citizens of EU countries, the European Free Trade Association (EFTA), and several other countries, including the United States, Canada, Australia, New Zealand, Japan, and South Korea, do not require a visa for short stays (up to 90 days) for tourism or business purposes.

Visitors from countries not included in the visa-exempt list should check with the Greek consulate or embassy in their home country for specific visa requirements. Typically, citizens from non-exempt countries will need to apply for a Schengen visa, which allows entry to all Schengen Area countries, including Greece.

Visa applications often require certain documents, such as a valid passport, passport-sized photos, proof of travel insurance, a detailed itinerary, proof of sufficient funds for the stay, and a confirmed return or onward ticket.

Schengen Visa Validity:

The Schengen visa is usually issued for short stays of up to 90 days within a 180-day period. Travelers must be mindful of this limitation to avoid overstaying their visa, as such violations can result in fines, deportation, and future entry restrictions.

Long-Term Stays and Residence Permits:

For those intending to stay in Greece for purposes other than tourism or business, such as for work, study, or family reunification, different visa and residence permit regulations may apply. It is essential to research and apply for the appropriate visa well in advance of travel.

Customs and Entry Regulations:

Upon arrival in Greece, travelers must comply with customs regulations, declaring any goods subject to import restrictions or taxation, such as large quantities of alcohol or tobacco products. Travelers should be aware that Greece, like other Schengen Area countries, maintains strict border controls to ensure the safety and security of all visitors and residents. As such, all passengers may be subject to thorough document checks upon entry.

Travel Insurance:

While not a formal entry requirement, it is highly recommended for all visitors to Greece to have comprehensive travel insurance. Travel insurance provides coverage for medical emergencies, trip cancellations or interruptions, lost or stolen belongings, and other unforeseen events that could otherwise disrupt travel plans.

Consulate or Embassy Contact Information:

It is wise to have the contact information for your home country's consulate or embassy in Greece in case of emergencies or unforeseen circumstances during your stay.

By carefully adhering to passport and visa requirements, travelers can ensure a smooth and hassle-free journey to Greece, allowing them to focus on exploring the country's enchanting landscapes, ancient sites, and vibrant culture. Always verify the latest entry regulations before departure, as requirements may change over time due to international developments or policy updates.

HEALTH AND SAFETY TRAVEL GUIDELINES

When traveling to any destination, including Greece, it's essential to prioritize your health and safety. While the COVID-19 pandemic may have subsided, other health risks and general travel precautions still apply. Here are important health and safety guidelines to consider:

Vaccinations and Medical Checkups:

Before traveling to Greece, ensure that you are up-to-date with routine vaccinations, such as measles, mumps, rubella, diphtheria, tetanus, pertussis, and influenza. Vaccinations protect both you and the local population from preventable diseases.

Traveler's Health Insurance:

While not mandatory, having comprehensive traveler's health insurance is highly recommended. Travel insurance can provide coverage for unexpected medical expenses, emergency medical evacuations, and trip cancellations or interruptions due to health-related issues.

Consulting a Healthcare Professional:

If you have any pre-existing medical conditions or concerns, consult your healthcare provider before traveling. They can offer personalized health advice and help you prepare for your journey.

Safe Food and Water Practices:

While Greece generally maintains high standards of food safety, it's essential to be cautious when consuming food and beverages, especially from street vendors. Opt for bottled water, avoid consuming undercooked or raw foods, and wash your hands before eating.

Protecting Yourself from Insect Bites:

In some areas of Greece, particularly during certain seasons, insects like mosquitoes may carry diseases. Use insect repellents and wear appropriate clothing to protect yourself from bites.

Sun Protection:

Greece enjoys abundant sunshine, so it's crucial to protect yourself from the sun's harmful rays. Use sunscreen with a high SPF, wear sunglasses and a wide-brimmed hat, and seek shade during the peak hours of sunlight.

Staying Hydrated:

Especially during hot weather and when engaging in physical activities, ensure that you stay hydrated by drinking plenty of water.

Responsible Use of Medications:

If you take prescription medications, ensure you have an adequate supply for the duration of your trip. Keep medications in their original containers, and carry a copy of the prescriptions with you.

Emergency Medical Services:

Greece has a well-developed healthcare system with medical facilities and pharmacies widely available. In case of a medical emergency, call the European emergency number 112.

Cultural Considerations:

Familiarize yourself with local customs and cultural norms, as well as any specific health-related customs or practices observed by the locals.

Public Health Measures:

Be mindful of any local public health measures or guidelines in place during your visit. While they may not be related to COVID-19, they could pertain to other health concerns.

By adhering to these health and safety guidelines, you can enjoy a memorable and worry-free trip to Greece, savoring its rich history, breathtaking landscapes, and warm hospitality while taking care of your well-being. Remember that health considerations are paramount to ensure a positive travel experience.

CURRENCY, LANGUAGE, AND COMMUNICATION

When traveling to Greece, it's essential to familiarize yourself with the country's currency, language, and communication practices to ensure a smooth and enjoyable experience. Here are some important details to keep in mind:

Currency:

The official currency of Greece is the Euro (€). It is denoted by the symbol "€" and is available in both coins and banknotes. Currency exchange services are widely available, including at airports, banks, and exchange offices. It's a good idea to carry some cash for smaller purchases, as not all places may accept credit or debit cards, especially in remote areas.

Language:

The official language of Greece is Greek. While English is widely spoken in major tourist areas, especially by those working in the tourism industry, learning a few basic Greek phrases can enhance your travel experience and show appreciation for the local culture. Simple greetings such as "hello" (γειά σας - yia sas) and "thank you" (ευχαριστώ - efharistó) go a long way in establishing rapport with the locals.

Communication:

Greece has a well-developed telecommunications network, and you'll find reliable mobile phone coverage in most urban and rural areas. International roaming services are available for travelers who wish to use their own mobile phones. Alternatively, you can purchase a local SIM card from various providers for data and call services.

Internet Access:

The majority of hotels, cafes, and restaurants offer free Wi-Fi access to customers. Additionally, you'll find internet cafes in popular tourist destinations where you can access the internet for a fee.

Electricity:

Greece uses the standard European two-pin plug with a voltage of 230V and a frequency of 50Hz. If your devices use a different type of plug or voltage, make sure to bring the necessary adapters and converters.

Time Zone:

Greece is in the Eastern European Time (EET) zone, which is UTC+2. During daylight saving time, it follows Eastern European Summer Time (EEST), UTC+3.

Public Etiquette:

Greeks value politeness and respect in social interactions. When meeting someone, a handshake is the common greeting. It's customary to address people using their titles (Mr., Mrs., or Miss) followed by their last names. Punctuality is appreciated in formal settings.

Tipping:

Tipping is not obligatory in Greece, as a service charge is often included in the bill. However, leaving a small tip for exceptional service is appreciated. If you choose to tip, rounding up the bill or leaving about 5-10% of the total amount is customary.

By being mindful of these currency, language, and communication practices, you'll find it easier to navigate through Greece, interact with the locals, and immerse yourself in the country's rich culture and history. Embracing these aspects of travel enhances cultural understanding and enriches your overall experience in this captivating Mediterranean destination.

SAFETY TIPS AND HEALTH CARE

When traveling to Greece, ensuring your safety and well-being is of utmost importance. Greece is generally a safe destination for tourists, but like any other place, it's essential to exercise caution and be aware of certain safety tips. Additionally, understanding the local healthcare system can provide peace of mind in case of any medical emergencies. Here are some valuable safety tips and insights into the health care system in Greece:

Safety Tips:

Emergency Numbers: The universal emergency number in Greece is 112. For police assistance, dial 100, and for medical emergencies, dial 166.

Stay Informed: Before traveling, it's wise to stay informed about the current political situation and any travel advisories issued by your home country's government. Keep yourself updated about local news and events during your stay.

Pickpocketing: While Greece is relatively safe, petty theft and pickpocketing can occur, especially in crowded tourist areas. Be vigilant in public places and keep your belongings secure, preferably in a crossbody bag or a money belt.

Natural Disasters: Greece is prone to earthquakes, particularly in the southern regions. Familiarize yourself with earthquake safety measures and follow instructions from local authorities in case of an emergency.

Beach Safety: If you plan to enjoy Greece's beautiful beaches, pay attention to flag warnings indicating water conditions. Swim only in designated swimming areas, and be cautious of strong currents and undertows.

Sun Protection: The Mediterranean sun can be intense, especially during the summer months. Always wear sunscreen, a hat, and sunglasses to protect yourself from harmful UV rays.

Respect Local Customs: Greeks take pride in their culture and traditions. Be respectful of local customs and dress codes, especially when visiting religious sites.

Health Care:

European Health Insurance Card (EHIC): If you are an EU citizen, carry your EHIC to access state-provided healthcare in Greece. The EHIC ensures you receive necessary medical treatment under the same conditions as Greek nationals.

Healthcare System: Greece has a public healthcare system that provides quality medical services. In larger cities and popular tourist destinations, you'll find public and private hospitals and clinics with English-speaking staff.

Travel Insurance: Non-EU citizens and EU citizens without an EHIC should obtain comprehensive travel insurance before their trip. Travel insurance can cover medical emergencies, repatriation, and other unforeseen events.

Prescription Medications: If you take prescription medications, ensure you have an adequate supply for the duration of your trip. Carry your medications in their original packaging, along with a copy of the prescription.

Insect Protection: In certain rural areas, mosquitoes may be prevalent during specific seasons. Use insect repellents and consider wearing long sleeves and pants during evenings outdoors.

Food and Water Safety: Greek cuisine is delightful, but be cautious of consuming food from street vendors and ensure your drinking water is bottled or properly treated.

By adhering to these safety tips and being prepared with essential health care information, you can fully enjoy your trip to Greece with confidence and peace of mind. Stay open to the country's rich cultural experiences and immerse yourself in the beauty and history that this enchanting Mediterranean destination has to offer.

LOCAL CUSTOMS AND ETIQUETTE

Understanding and respecting the local customs and etiquette is essential when visiting Greece. Greek culture is deeply rooted in tradition and hospitality, and adhering to certain practices will not only make your interactions smoother but also show your appreciation for the country's heritage. Here are some important customs and etiquette tips to keep in mind during your travels in Greece:

Greetings and Gestures:

Handshakes: A firm handshake is the common form of greeting in Greece, both in social and professional settings. Maintain eye contact and smile during the greeting.

Kisses on the Cheek: In more informal situations, especially between friends and family, it is customary to exchange kisses on both cheeks. However, it is not obligatory, so follow the lead of the locals.

Politeness and Respect

Formal Address: Greeks are generally polite and appreciate the use of formal titles such as "Mr." (Kyrios) and "Mrs." (Kyria) followed by the person's last name.

Use "Please" and "Thank You": Politeness goes a long way in Greek culture. Remember to use "parakaló" (please) and "efcharistó" (thank you) regularly.

Dress Code:

Be Respectful: Greece is a conservative country, especially in rural areas and religious sites. Dress modestly when visiting churches and monasteries, covering your shoulders and wearing knee-length or longer clothing.

Beach Attire: While swimwear is acceptable on the beaches, avoid walking around town in your bathing suit.

Tipping:

Service Charge: In restaurants and cafes, a service charge is often included in the bill. However, it's customary to leave a small tip (around 5% to 10%) for exceptional service.

Taxi Drivers: Tipping taxi drivers is not mandatory, but rounding up the fare or leaving small change is a common practice.

Respect Religious Sites:

Church Etiquette: When entering an Orthodox Church, both men and women should dress modestly. Avoid wearing hats, and women should cover their hair with a scarf. Maintain a respectful silence and refrain from using flash photography during religious services.

Toasting and Drinking:

Toasting: Greeks love to toast and celebrate with a hearty "Yamas!" (cheers). Make eye contact with each person while clinking glasses.

Drinking Laws: The legal drinking age in Greece is 18. Public drinking and drunken behavior are frowned upon.

Language Considerations:

Learn Basic Greek Phrases: While English is widely spoken, making an effort to learn some basic Greek phrases such as "hello" (yassas), "please" (parakaló), and "thank you" (efcharistó) will be appreciated by the locals.

Queuing and Personal Space:

Patience in Lines: Be patient when queuing for attractions or services, as lines may not always be as structured as you're used to.

Personal Space: Greeks are generally friendly and may stand closer to you during conversations. Personal space boundaries might be different, but feel free to politely step back if you feel uncomfortable.

By embracing these local customs and showing respect for Greek traditions, you'll find yourself warmly welcomed by the locals and have a more enriching cultural experience during your stay in Greece. Remember, a genuine interest in the country's customs and a willingness to adapt will surely be reciprocated with Greek hospitality and fond memories of your trip.

CHAPTER 5 - TRANSPORTATION GUIDE

Greece offers a variety of transportation options for travelers to explore its diverse landscapes, from ancient ruins to picturesque islands. Navigating the transportation system efficiently will enhance your overall travel experience. Here's a comprehensive guide to getting around Greece:

AIR TRAVEL AND AIRPORTS IN GREECE

Major Airports:

Athens International Airport (ATH): Located in the capital city, Athens International Airport, also known as Eleftherios Venizelos, is the largest and busiest airport in Greece. It serves as the primary gateway to the country, offering numerous international and domestic flights.

Thessaloniki International Airport (SKG): Situated in northern Greece, Thessaloniki Airport is the second-largest airport in the country, providing both domestic and international flights.

Regional Airports:

Heraklion International Airport (HER): Serving Crete, this airport connects the island to various domestic and European destinations.

Santorini (Thira) International Airport (JTR): Located on the popular island of Santorini, this airport operates seasonal flights from major European cities.

Mykonos International Airport (JMK): Serving the vibrant island of Mykonos, this airport connects to several European cities during the peak tourist season.

Rhodes International Airport (RHO): Situated on the island of Rhodes, this airport offers flights to and from major European cities.

Corfu International Airport (CFU): Serving the lush island of Corfu, this airport connects to various European destinations.

Chania International Airport (CHQ): Located in Crete, Chania Airport operates seasonal flights to and from European cities.

Domestic Flights:

Domestic flights in Greece are convenient for traveling between the mainland and the islands or between different islands. They are operated by several airlines, including Aegean Airlines and Olympic Air.

Flights to popular tourist destinations, such as Santorini, Mykonos, and Crete, can get fully booked quickly during peak travel seasons, so it's advisable to book in advance.

Getting to and from Airports:

Athens: The Athens airport is well-connected to the city center by public transportation, including the metro, buses, and taxis. The metro ride to the city center takes around 40 minutes.

Thessaloniki: The airport is approximately 15 km from the city center, and you can reach it by public buses or taxis.

Travel Tips:

Arrive Early: To avoid any last-minute hassles, especially during peak travel times, it's advisable to arrive at the airport well in advance.

Luggage Considerations: Pay attention to luggage restrictions and weight allowances for both international and domestic flights, as they may vary among different airlines.

COVID-19 Safety Measures:

As of 2023, the COVID-19 pandemic is no longer a concern, and Greece, like many other countries, has successfully managed to control and overcome the virus. Travelers are no longer required to follow specific COVID-19 safety measures, such as wearing masks, social distancing, or providing vaccination certificates.

However, it's always advisable to stay informed about any general health and safety guidelines that may be in place during your visit to Greece. It's essential to be aware of any potential health risks associated with traveling to a foreign country and take necessary precautions as advised by local health authorities.

Travelers are encouraged to have regular vaccinations, keep up-to-date with any necessary booster shots, and maintain good personal hygiene practices during their travels. It's also a good idea to have travel insurance that covers any potential medical needs while abroad.

Always check the latest travel advisories and guidelines issued by your home country's government regarding international travel to Greece. By staying informed and prepared, you can ensure a safe and enjoyable trip to this historically and culturally rich Mediterranean destination.

Greece offers a well-developed and efficient transportation network that makes it easy for travelers to explore various regions of the country. From bustling cities to quaint villages and picturesque islands, there are several transportation options available for inter-city travel.

Trains: Greece has an extensive railway system operated by Hellenic Railways Organization (OSE), connecting major cities and towns. Train travel in Greece is known for its scenic routes, providing travelers with beautiful views of the countryside. However, the train network might not cover all destinations, especially on the islands, where other modes of transportation are more common.

Buses: Buses are a popular and cost-effective way to travel between cities and towns in Greece. KTEL is the primary bus company in the country, offering regular services to various destinations. Buses are comfortable and air-conditioned, making them a convenient choice for travelers. Additionally, buses are often the only mode of public transportation available on the islands, providing connectivity between towns and tourist attractions.

Ferries: Since Greece is famous for its numerous islands, ferries play a crucial role in inter-island transportation. Several ferry companies operate routes between the mainland and the islands, as well as between different islands. High-speed ferries are available for popular tourist destinations and offer a quicker journey. On the other hand, conventional ferries provide a more relaxed and scenic experience, allowing travelers to enjoy the beauty of the Aegean Sea.

Flights: For long-distance travel between major cities and islands, domestic flights are available. Aegean Airlines and other regional carriers offer frequent flights to popular destinations, providing a time-saving option for those who want to cover significant distances quickly. Additionally, some remote islands are accessible only by air, making flights the most efficient means of transportation.

Renting a Car: Renting a car is an excellent option for travelers who prefer more flexibility and independence during their trip. Greece has a well-maintained road network, and driving allows visitors to explore off-the-beaten-path destinations and enjoy scenic drives. However, driving in busy city centers might be challenging, and parking can be limited, so it's advisable to use public transportation within cities.

Taxi Services: Taxis are widely available in major cities and tourist areas. While they can be more expensive than other forms of public transportation, they are a convenient option for short trips or when you need to travel at odd hours.

When planning your inter-city travels in Greece, consider the duration, cost, and convenience of each transportation mode. For island-hopping adventures, check the ferry schedules in advance, as they can vary depending on the season. By combining different transportation options strategically, you can create an itinerary that allows you to make the most of your Greek journey.

CAR RENTALS AND DRIVING IN GREECE

Renting a car in Greece can be a fantastic way to explore the country at your own pace and access off-the-beaten-path destinations. However, it's essential to be well-informed and prepared for driving in Greece to ensure a safe and enjoyable experience.

Choosing a Rental Car: When selecting a rental car, consider the size and type that best suits your travel needs. For navigating narrow village streets and parking in crowded city centers, a compact car is often more practical. If you plan to venture into the countryside or travel with a group, a larger car or even a minivan might be a better option.

Driving Regulations: To rent and drive a car in Greece, you must be at least 21 years old and possess a valid driver's license from your home country. An International Driving Permit (IDP) is recommended, although not mandatory. Always carry your passport, driver's license, and car rental documents with you while driving.

Driving Laws and Safety: Driving in Greece follows the right-hand traffic rule, and seat belts are compulsory for all passengers. Children under 10 must sit in the back seat, and it's the driver's responsibility to ensure they are using appropriate child restraints. The use of mobile phones while driving is strictly prohibited unless you have a hands-free system.

Road Conditions: Greek roads range from well-maintained highways to narrow, winding village roads. While major highways are generally in good condition, some rural roads might have potholes or uneven surfaces. Exercise caution when driving on unfamiliar roads, especially during the night, and be aware of local driving habits.

Parking: Parking in urban areas can be challenging, so it's advisable to use public transportation within cities whenever possible. When parking on the street, ensure that you follow the designated parking signs and avoid obstructing traffic. In some areas, paid parking zones are enforced, and fines may apply for violations.

Fuel Stations: Gas stations are readily available in urban areas and along major highways. Most stations offer unleaded (95 and 100 octane) and diesel fuel. Some stations may close during the late evening hours, so plan your fuel stops accordingly.

Navigating Greek Roads: While driving, pay attention to road signs, especially those indicating speed limits and directions to major cities and tourist attractions. GPS and mobile navigation apps can be helpful tools for getting around, but it's also a good idea to have a physical map on hand as a backup.

Driving in Cities: Driving in cities like Athens and Thessaloniki can be challenging due to heavy traffic and narrow streets. Be patient, stay alert, and be cautious of pedestrians and other drivers. If you prefer not to drive in busy city centers, consider using public transportation or taxis.

Driving in Rural Areas: In rural areas, be prepared for encounters with slow-moving agricultural vehicles and livestock on the roads. Exercise extra caution, especially when driving around blind curves and hilly terrain.

By familiarizing yourself with Greek driving regulations and road conditions, you can confidently embark on a road trip through the stunning landscapes of Greece and create lasting memories of your journey. Always prioritize safety and obey local traffic laws to ensure a smooth and enjoyable travel experience.

FERRIES AND ISLAND HOPPING

Island hopping is a quintessential experience for anyone visiting Greece. With thousands of islands scattered across the Aegean and Ionian Seas, ferries play a crucial role in connecting these beautiful destinations. Here's everything you need to know about ferries and island hopping in Greece:

Types of Ferries: Greece offers various types of ferries, ranging from large, modern vessels to smaller, more traditional boats. The type of ferry you choose will depend on the distance between islands and your personal preferences. Common ferry types include:

High-Speed Ferries: These modern vessels are faster and more expensive than regular ferries. They are ideal for covering long distances between major islands quickly.

Conventional Ferries: These larger, slower ferries are more budget-friendly and suitable for shorter journeys. They are equipped with amenities such as restaurants, lounges, and outdoor decks.

Local Ferries: Smaller, traditional boats that connect smaller islands and less touristy destinations. They offer a more authentic and intimate island-hopping experience.

Ferry Schedules and Tickets: Ferry schedules in Greece can vary based on the season, demand, and specific routes. During the peak summer months, it's advisable to book your ferry tickets in advance, especially if you have a fixed travel itinerary. Tickets can be purchased online through official ferry company websites or at the ports. Arriving early before departure is recommended, as boarding can get crowded, especially for popular routes.

Island Hopping Routes: Popular island-hopping routes include the Cyclades, Dodecanese, Ionian Islands, and the Saronic Gulf Islands. Each island group offers its unique charm, landscape, and attractions. For example:

The Cyclades boast iconic destinations like Mykonos, Santorini, and Paros, known for their stunning beaches, vibrant nightlife, and traditional architecture.

The Dodecanese islands, including Rhodes and Kos, offer a blend of historical landmarks and pristine coastlines.

The Ionian Islands, such as Corfu and Zakynthos, are famous for their lush greenery, turquoise waters, and Venetian influence.

Purchasing Island Passes: For travelers planning to visit multiple islands within a specific region, some ferry companies offer island passes, providing flexibility and cost savings. These passes allow you to hop on and off ferries within a set period, making island hopping more convenient and affordable.

Additional Tips for Island Hopping:

Pack Light: Be mindful of luggage size and weight restrictions on ferries, as you might need to carry your bags up and down ramps during boarding.

Be Weather-Aware: Sea conditions can be unpredictable, especially during the windy season. If you are prone to seasickness, consider choosing larger, more stable ferries or alternative transportation options.

Plan for Ample Time: Island hopping can be time-consuming, so allocate enough time for each island to explore and fully enjoy its attractions.

Local Connections: Embrace interactions with locals, as they can offer valuable insights into lesser-known gems and authentic experiences.

Island hopping in Greece is a remarkable way to discover the country's diverse landscapes, culture, and history. With careful planning and a sense of adventure, your island-hopping journey is sure to be a memorable and enriching travel experience.

CHAPTER 6 - ACCOMMODATION

Your temporary abode while travelling plays a pivotal role in shaping your overall journey. It becomes more than just a place to sleep—it turns into your home away from home. The spectrum of accommodations, from cozy budget hostels, charming mid-range hotels to opulent luxury resorts, caters to varied tastes, providing distinctive experiences and connections to your destination.

In this chapter, we illuminate the intricate aspects of accommodations, equipping you with practical tips and innovative tactics to sift through an array of choices. Our focus extends beyond conventional options; we delve into unique lodgings that create an immersive cultural connection with the locale you visit.

We address aspects to enhance your booking experience and maximize your stay, considering key elements like location, facilities, service quality, and cost-effectiveness. We also guide you on aligning accommodation choices with your financial plan and travel persona. Our suggestions encompass the wide-ranging needs of travelers, from solo wanderers craving a lively hostel vibe to families seeking the conveniences of a well-equipped hotel, or couples in pursuit of the opulence of a luxury villa.

In the context of Greece, we delve into distinctive accommodations that authentically encapsulate Greek living. The country abounds with unique experiences, from mountainous stone mansions to Aegean-facing whitewashed villas. These enrich your journey by offering a taste of the local lifestyle.

With the insights from this chapter, you'll navigate the accommodation landscape with greater confidence, making choices that enhance your travel experience and align with your unique travel narrative.

TIPS FOR BOOKING ACCOMMODATION

Securing a fitting abode during your Greek odyssey can significantly amplify your comfort and satisfaction levels. As you map out your expedition, these strategies can help optimize your accommodation arrangements:

1. **Plan Ahead:** Especially during the peak tourist season, it's advisable to book your accommodation well in advance. This ensures you have a wide range of options and can secure the best deals.

2. **Choose the Right Location:** Consider the purpose of your trip and the activities you wish to pursue. If you're interested in exploring historical sites, staying in the heart of Athens might be ideal. On the other hand, if you're looking for a relaxing beach vacation, opting for a seaside resort on an island is a great choice.

3. **Read Reviews and Ratings:** Before making a reservation, take the time to read reviews from previous guests. Websites like TripAdvisor, Booking.com, or Airbnb provide valuable insights into the quality and services offered by different accommodations.

4. **Consider Your Budget:** Greece offers a wide range of accommodation options to suit various budgets. Determine how much you are willing to spend on accommodation and look for options that fit within your budget without compromising on quality and comfort.

5. **Authentic Experiences:** To immerse yourself in the local culture, consider staying in boutique hotels, guesthouses, or traditional villas. These accommodations often offer a more authentic experience and a chance to connect with the local community.

6. **Amenities and Services:** Check the amenities provided by the accommodation, such as Wi-Fi availability, air conditioning, breakfast options, and parking facilities. Make sure the chosen place meets your specific needs and preferences.

7. **Flexible Booking Options:** Given the unpredictable nature of travel, opt for accommodations that offer flexible booking policies. This will allow you to make changes to your reservation without incurring significant fees.

8. **Consider the Season:** The time of year you visit Greece can impact accommodation availability and prices. During the high season (summer), prices may be higher, and popular places tend to book up quickly. If you prefer a quieter experience and better rates, consider visiting during the shoulder season.

9. **Local Recommendations:** Reach out to locals or travel forums to seek recommendations on hidden gems or lesser-known accommodations that may not be widely advertised online.

10. **Book Directly:** While third-party booking platforms are convenient, sometimes booking directly with the accommodation can lead to better rates and additional perks or upgrades.

11. **Safety and Cleanliness:** In light of the COVID-19 pandemic, ensure that the accommodation follows proper health and safety protocols to provide a clean and safe environment for guests.

By considering these tips, you can make well-informed decisions when booking accommodation in Greece. Whether you're seeking luxury resorts, charming guesthouses, or budget-friendly hostels, Greece offers a diverse range of options to suit every traveler's needs and preferences.

BUDGET, MID-RANGE, AND LUXURY OPTIONS

Greece caters to a wide range of travelers, offering diverse accommodation options to suit different budgets and preferences. Here's a breakdown of the various categories of accommodations available:

1. Budget Options:

- Hostels: Ideal for budget-conscious travelers and backpackers, hostels provide shared dormitory-style rooms with communal facilities. They offer an excellent opportunity to meet fellow travelers and often include common areas and communal kitchens. Some hostels may also have private rooms for those seeking a bit more privacy.

- Guesthouses and Pensions: These small family-run establishments offer a more intimate setting than hostels. Guesthouses provide private rooms at affordable prices, often with basic amenities. Staying in a guesthouse allows you to experience warm Greek hospitality and immerse yourself in the local culture.

- Budget Hotels: Greece has a variety of budget hotels that offer comfortable rooms and essential amenities at affordable rates. While not as luxurious as high-end hotels, budget hotels provide a convenient and budget-friendly option for travelers.

2. Mid-range Options:

- 3 to 4-star Hotels: Mid-range hotels in Greece offer a good balance between comfort and affordability. They provide well-appointed rooms, often with additional amenities such as swimming pools, on-site restaurants, and fitness centers. These hotels are suitable for travelers seeking a comfortable stay without splurging on luxury.

- Boutique Hotels: For a more unique and personalized experience, consider boutique hotels. These intimate properties are characterized by their distinctive architecture, stylish decor, and attention to detail. Boutique hotels often have fewer rooms, ensuring a more exclusive atmosphere.

- Traditional Villas: In certain regions, you can find traditional villas available for rent. These charming properties showcase local architecture and offer a sense of authenticity. Renting a villa is an excellent choice for families or groups looking for privacy and independence.

3. Luxury Options:

- 5-star Hotels and Resorts: Greece boasts numerous luxury hotels and resorts that provide world-class facilities and services. Expect elegant and spacious rooms, upscale dining options, spa facilities, and breathtaking views. Many luxury properties are situated in idyllic locations, such as private beaches or overlooking the Aegean Sea.

- Private Villas and Suites: For the ultimate luxury experience, consider booking a private villa or suite in a high-end resort. These accommodations often come with exclusive services, private pools, and direct access to the beach.

- Historic Mansions and Palaces: In some destinations, historic mansions and palaces have been converted into luxurious hotels, offering a glimpse into Greece's rich heritage. Staying in one of these opulent properties provides a unique and unforgettable experience.

Regardless of the category you choose, it's essential to research and read reviews to ensure that the accommodation aligns with your expectations. Booking in advance, especially during peak seasons, is advisable, as popular places tend to fill up quickly. Keep in mind the location and proximity to attractions or activities you plan to explore, as well as any specific amenities or services that are important to you. Greece's diverse range of accommodations ensures that every traveler can find the perfect place to stay and create lasting memories during their Greek adventure.

UNIQUE ACCOMMODATION EXPERIENCES IN GREECE

Beyond the traditional options of hotels and resorts, Greece offers a plethora of unique accommodation experiences that allow travelers to immerse themselves in the country's rich history, natural beauty, and authentic culture. These distinctive stays provide an extraordinary and unforgettable way to explore Greece:

1. Historic Guesthouses: Stay in lovingly restored historic buildings, such as old manors, monasteries, or traditional stone houses. These guesthouses often preserve their original charm while offering modern comforts. By choosing a historic guesthouse, you can indulge in the country's architectural heritage and connect with its past.

2. Agritourism Farms: Experience rural Greece by staying at an agritourism farm. These rustic properties allow you to witness traditional farming practices, participate in activities like olive harvesting, and savor farm-to-table meals with locally sourced ingredients. Agritourism accommodations offer an authentic escape into Greece's countryside and agricultural traditions.

3. Cave Hotels: Several Greek islands, such as Santorini and Milos, offer cave hotels carved into volcanic rock formations. These unique dwellings boast stunning views of the caldera and Aegean Sea. Staying in a cave hotel provides a romantic and distinctive experience amidst breathtaking natural surroundings.

4. Traditional Sailboats: Embark on a seafaring adventure by opting for a stay on a traditional wooden sailboat, known as a "caique." These vessels are equipped with comfortable cabins and offer island-hopping cruises, providing a novel way to explore the Greek islands from the sea.

5. Treehouses and Eco-Lodges: For eco-conscious travelers, Greece boasts several eco-lodges and treehouses that blend seamlessly with nature. These sustainable accommodations provide an off-the-grid experience, surrounded by lush landscapes and wildlife.

6. Themed Suites: Some luxury hotels and resorts in Greece feature themed suites inspired by Greek mythology, history, or culture. Indulge in a stay fit for the gods, surrounded by opulent decor and exclusive amenities.

7. Lighthouses: A few lighthouses along the Greek coastline have been converted into unique accommodations, offering unparalleled views of the sea and coastline. These remote and atmospheric locations provide a peaceful retreat away from the hustle and bustle.

8. Glamping: Experience the best of nature without compromising on comfort by opting for glamping (glamorous camping). Stay in luxurious tents or yurts nestled in picturesque landscapes, such as near national parks or sandy beaches.

9. Underwater Hotels: For a truly one-of-a-kind experience, consider staying in an underwater hotel suite, available in some regions with crystal-clear waters. Enjoy a mesmerizing view of marine life and the ocean floor from the comfort of your room.

10. Contemporary Art Hotels: Greece's cultural scene extends to its accommodations, with some hotels featuring contemporary art installations and design. Immerse yourself in creativity and aesthetics while exploring the local artistic expression.

Remember to book these unique accommodations well in advance, as they often have limited availability due to their exclusivity. Whether you choose to stay in a historic guesthouse, a traditional sailboat, or a glamping site, these unique accommodation experiences will add a special touch to your journey through Greece, creating memories that will last a lifetime.

"GOOD WILL"

YOUR FEEDBACK MATTERS!

Did you enjoy the book? We would be grateful if you could leave an honest review on Amazon. If there's something you didn't like, we would appreciate your constructive feedback. Please send your suggestions to stevanclark.author@gmail.com.

Your input will help improve future editions of this book and will be highly appreciated.

MAKE A DIFFERENCE, LEAVE AN HONEST REVIEW

If this book added value to your life, please consider sharing your honest opinion in a review. It takes just 30 seconds but can provide invaluable insights for others.

HOW TO LEAVE A REVIEW

- For E-readers: Swipe up on the last page to bring up the review window.
- For Paperback: Visit the Amazon page of the book to leave your review.

THANK YOU

Your support is invaluable. From the bottom of my heart, thank you.

Stevan Clark

Chapter 7 - Greek Language Guide: Engage Deeper with the Local Culture

*W*elcome, fellow globetrotters, to the exciting world of the Greek language. If you're looking to venture beyond the "kalimera" and "efharisto" you learned from our travel essentials chapter, then you've come to the right place! Let's dive into some common Greek phrases and terms that will surely endear you to the locals and enrich your travel experience.

The Greek Alphabet

Before we start, a quick introduction to the Greek alphabet would be helpful. Many letters may look familiar, as they are used in scientific notations and college fraternities. Don't worry about perfection. The goal here is to feel a little more at home when you see Greek words written out.

Essential Phrases:

Dive in the pool of Greek language with these common phrases. Don't worry about sounding perfect - it's the effort that counts!

1. *"Kalimera"* (Good Morning) - A cheerful way to start your day!
2. *"Kali Spera"* (Good Evening) - Greet the enchanting Greek evenings with this phrase.
3. *"Ti kanis?"* (How are you?) - Shows the locals that you're interested in their well-being.
4. *"Signomi"* (Excuse me) - Essential for navigating through the bustling Athenian streets or getting a waiter's attention.
5. *"Parakalo"* (Please/You're welcome) - Politeness is valued universally!
6. *"Stin iyia mas!"* (Cheers/To our health) - You'll surely be using this a lot when you explore Greece's amazing tavernas.
7. *"Pou einai i toualeta?"* (Where is the bathroom?) - Handy in case of emergencies.
8. *"Thelo ena tiketo gia..."* (I want a ticket to...) - Useful when using public transportation or visiting tourist spots.

Local Slang:

If you want to sound less like a tourist and more like a local, try adding these slang words to your vocabulary:

1. *"Malaka"* - A term of endearment among friends, though be careful with the context, as it can be offensive if used wrongly.

2. *"Kefi"* - This word embodies the Greek zest for life. It's often used to describe good spirits or fun atmosphere.

3. *"Frappe"* - Not exactly slang, but very important. It's the national coffee of Greece!

4. *"Parea"* - This means company or group, typically referring to a group of friends hanging out.

Understanding Greek Gestures:

Language isn't just about the words we say; it's also about body language and gestures. Here are a couple you might notice:

1. *"Moutza"* - Open palm displayed outward or towards someone. Be careful, it's considered a serious insult.

2. *Nodding and shaking the head* - In Greece, a slight downward nod means 'yes', and a slight shake of the head to the sides means 'no'. Quite the reverse of many other cultures, so it can be a bit confusing at first!

Engaging with Locals:

Now you have some basic Greek phrases and cultural understanding in your toolkit. It's time to step out and engage with the locals. Don't be shy! Most Greeks are friendly and would appreciate your efforts to speak their language.

So, there you have it. A little guide to help you navigate the language landscape of Greece. Remember, language is the road map of a culture. It tells you where its people come from and where they are going. Enjoy your journey in Greece, and who knows? You might come back speaking Greek like a local!

In our next chapter, we will uncover more fascinating aspects of Greek culture, so stay tuned!

Note: *This guide is intended to break the ice and help you understand and engage in basic Greek conversation. If you're looking to delve deeper into the language, consider enrolling in a formal language course or using a language learning app. Also, Greeks are usually fluent in English, especially in urban and touristic areas, so don't stress too much about mastering Greek. Enjoy your trip!*

CHAPTER 8 - EXPLORING ATHENS

*A*ncient and modern, chaotic yet charming, Athens is a city of paradoxes that beckons travelers with its rich history, vibrant culture, and a lively food scene. The sprawling metropolis is a treasure trove of historic sites, fascinating museums, bustling markets, and inviting eateries, all waiting to be discovered. In this chapter, we embark on a virtual exploration of Athens, guiding you through its labyrinthine streets and shedding light on its intriguing character. We delve into an overview of the city, providing key insights that will set the stage for your Athenian adventure. We journey back in time, visiting Athens' celebrated historic sites and museums, where relics of the past whisper tales of glory and grandeur. From the awe-inspiring Acropolis to the insightful National Archaeological Museum, we delve into the heart of Greece's historic and cultural heritage.

Food is central to the Greek way of life, and in Athens, the culinary scene is a delectable blend of tradition and innovation. We'll guide you through local cuisine and the array of dining options, from charming tavernas serving soulful homemade dishes to elegant restaurants offering modern twists on classic recipes.

Finally, we'll guide you through the vibrant shopping landscape of Athens, where local markets brim with artisanal crafts, and upscale stores showcase the best of Greek design.

Immerse yourself in this chapter to gain a well-rounded understanding of Athens and its abundant offerings, providing a solid foundation for your impending journey.

OVERVIEW OF ATHENS

As the capital of Greece and one of the world's oldest cities, Athens holds a captivating mix of ancient history and modern vibrancy. This bustling metropolis offers travelers a remarkable journey through time, where ancient ruins coexist harmoniously with contemporary architecture and vibrant neighborhoods. Here's an overview of what you can expect when exploring Athens:

Historical Marvels: Athens is home to some of the most significant archaeological sites in the world. The Acropolis, a UNESCO World Heritage site, stands proudly atop a rocky hill overlooking the city. Dominated by the iconic Parthenon, this ancient citadel showcases the brilliance of Classical Greek architecture. Other noteworthy historical sites include the Ancient Agora, the Temple of Olympian Zeus, and the Roman Agora.

Museums and Cultural Gems: Immerse yourself in Greece's rich history and art by visiting the city's exceptional museums. The Acropolis Museum houses an impressive collection of artifacts found on the Acropolis site, offering invaluable insights into ancient Greek civilization. The National Archaeological Museum is another must-visit, displaying an extensive collection of antiquities from various regions of Greece.

Cosmopolitan Neighborhoods: Athens is a city of diverse neighborhoods, each with its unique character and allure. Plaka, known as the "Neighborhood of the Gods," features charming narrow streets, neoclassical buildings, and an array of tavernas and shops. Monastiraki is renowned for its bustling flea market and vibrant atmosphere, while Kolonaki caters to upscale shopping and dining experiences.

Culinary Delights: Greek cuisine is a delightful culinary journey, and Athens is the perfect place to savor its authentic flavors. Taste mouthwatering souvlaki, freshly caught seafood, and delicious Mediterranean salads. Don't miss trying traditional Greek sweets like baklava and loukoumades. As night falls, join the locals at a taverna for a memorable dining experience accompanied by live music.

Mount Lycabettus: For panoramic views of Athens, take a leisurely hike or ride the funicular to the top of Mount Lycabettus. From its peak, you can enjoy breathtaking vistas of the entire city, stretching all the way to the Aegean Sea.

Vibrant Nightlife: Athens comes alive at night, offering a vibrant nightlife scene that caters to all tastes. Whether you prefer sipping cocktails at rooftop bars with views of the illuminated Acropolis or dancing the night away in lively nightclubs, Athens has something to suit every mood.

Green Oases: Despite its urban hustle, Athens boasts several green spaces where you can unwind and escape the city's buzz. The National Garden and Zappeion Garden are perfect for a leisurely stroll amidst lush greenery, while the Stavros Niarchos Foundation Cultural Center combines culture and nature with its expansive park and cultural venues.

Contemporary Art and Culture: Athens has emerged as a hub for contemporary art, with numerous art galleries and cultural centers. Explore the Gazi district for its vibrant art scene, or visit the Benaki Museum for contemporary Greek art exhibitions.

Exploring Athens is like stepping into a living history book. The city's ancient wonders, diverse neighborhoods, flavorful cuisine, and vibrant culture create an unforgettable travel experience. As you traverse its streets and discover its secrets, Athens will undoubtedly leave an indelible mark on your heart.

GETTING AROUND ATHENS: A DETAILED GUIDE TO THE CITY'S TRANSPORTATION

Navigating a new city can feel like unraveling an ancient labyrinth, especially in a city as old as Athens. The birthplace of democracy might not be your first thought when you think of modern, streamlined public transport. However, Athens boasts an impressively efficient transportation network that will whisk you from the bustling heart of the city to the edge of the Aegean Sea. In this chapter, we'll explore the main ways to get around Athens, from the depths of the metro system to the scenic tram routes and even cycling paths for those who prefer a more hands-on approach.

THE METRO: AN UNDERGROUND ODYSSEY

The Athens Metro is a testament to the city's marriage of ancient history and modern efficiency. Consisting of three lines (Line 1: Green, Line 2: Red, and Line 3: Blue), the metro covers a large part of the city and its suburbs. While you won't catch sight of the Parthenon from the underground, what you do get is a speedy, punctual, and air-conditioned journey to your destination.

Uniquely, several metro stations double as mini-museums. As the metro tunnels were dug, ancient artifacts were uncovered and are now displayed in the stations. So don't rush too much—you might just pass by some thousands-of-years-old pottery on your way to the platform!

BUSES & TROLLEYBUSES: JOURNEYS ABOVE GROUND

If you'd rather keep your travels above ground where you can soak up the cityscape, Athens' extensive bus and trolleybus networks will be more your speed. They cover the entire city and also offer routes to the greater Attica region. The bus system can be a bit more complex to navigate, but the payoff is worth it. From the winding city streets to the mountainous outskirts, these buses have it all.

THE TRAM: A SCENIC COASTAL CRUISE

The Athens Tram system is your ticket to the Greek seaside. It connects the city center with the southern coastal suburbs, offering stunning views of the Saronic Gulf. It's the perfect way to travel to the beaches around Alimos and Glyfada while enjoying the scenery en route. Remember to bring your camera, as the sun setting over the Aegean Sea is a sight you'll want to capture!

TAXIS AND RIDESHARES: DOOR-TO-DOOR CONVENIENCE

Taxis are abundant in Athens and, compared to many other European cities, quite affordable. It's a convenient option, especially if you're traveling in a group or have a lot of luggage. In addition to traditional taxis, rideshare apps like Beat (the Greek equivalent of Uber) are widely used.

BIKES: PEDAL POWER

In recent years, Athens has been gradually becoming more bicycle-friendly, with bike lanes appearing in the city center and a bike-sharing scheme in operation. It's an eco-friendly way to explore the city at your own pace, especially attractive in areas like the National Gardens or the coastal promenade.

WALKING: AT YOUR OWN PACE

Finally, never underestimate the power of your own two feet. Athens' city center is packed with history and is relatively compact, making it ideal for exploring on foot. After all, what could be better than stumbling upon an ancient monument on your leisurely stroll?

As with any city, when using public transportation in Athens, remain aware of your belongings, respect the local etiquette, and validate your tickets to avoid fines. With this guide, you're well-equipped to navigate Athens like a local. Now, let's embark on our journey through this enchanting city—next stop, adventure!

HISTORIC SITES AND MUSEUMS

Athens, with its rich history dating back over 3,000 years, boasts an array of historic sites and world-class museums that provide a captivating glimpse into ancient Greek civilization and beyond. Immerse yourself in the fascinating stories and cultural heritage as you explore these remarkable attractions:

The Acropolis: Undoubtedly the crown jewel of Athens, the Acropolis is an ancient citadel perched high above the city. Marvel at the architectural brilliance of the Parthenon, dedicated to the goddess Athena, and the Erechtheion, an exquisite temple with its iconic Caryatids. As you walk among these iconic ruins, you'll feel a profound connection to the ancient world.

The Acropolis Museum: Located near the Acropolis, the Acropolis Museum is a modern marvel housing a vast collection of archaeological finds. The museum's exhibits beautifully narrate the history of the Acropolis, showcasing artifacts dating from the Archaic to the Roman period. Don't miss the glass floor revealing the ancient city's remains beneath your feet.

Ancient Agora: Step into the heart of ancient Athenian life at the Ancient Agora, the city's marketplace and civic center. Explore the ruins of various public buildings, temples, and stoas that once bustled with commercial and philosophical activities. The well-preserved Temple of Hephaestus stands as a testament to Doric architecture.

National Archaeological Museum: Delve into the world's most extensive collection of Greek antiquities at the National Archaeological Museum. This vast repository houses over 11,000 exhibits, including fascinating artifacts from Mycenaean, Cycladic, and Minoan cultures. Admire the Antikythera Mechanism, an ancient analog computer, and the hauntingly beautiful bronze statue of Poseidon.

Temple of Olympian Zeus: Witness the grandeur of the Temple of Olympian Zeus, once the largest temple in ancient Greece. Although largely in ruins, its towering Corinthian columns and remnants provide a sense of the temple's former magnificence.

Kerameikos Archaeological Site: Uncover the ancient cemetery and ceremonial grounds at the Kerameikos Archaeological Site. Discover well-preserved grave markers and tombs that offer insight into ancient burial customs and rituals.

Benaki Museum: For a comprehensive understanding of Greek culture and history, the Benaki Museum is a must-visit. The museum's diverse exhibits span from prehistoric times to modern Greece, encompassing art, artifacts, and historical objects.

Byzantine and Christian Museum: Explore the heritage of the Byzantine Empire and early Christianity at this exceptional museum. Exhibits include religious artifacts, icons, mosaics, and precious manuscripts.

Museum of Cycladic Art: Delight in the elegant simplicity of Cycladic art, characterized by its abstract and minimalist forms. This museum houses an impressive collection of Cycladic figurines and artifacts.

Numismatic Museum: Trace the history of currency in Greece and beyond at the Numismatic Museum. The collection includes ancient coins, medals, and banknotes, providing a unique perspective on economic and cultural evolution.

Theatre of Dionysus: Uncover the birthplace of Western theater at the Theatre of Dionysus. Nestled on the southern slope of the Acropolis, this ancient amphitheater once hosted the dramatic works of legendary playwrights like Sophocles and Euripides.

Embark on a captivating journey through time as you explore Athens' historic sites and museums. Each location holds a wealth of knowledge, cultural significance, and architectural splendor, making your visit a profound and enriching experience. Remember to plan your itinerary wisely, as the sheer wealth of history and art might leave you longing to linger at every turn.

LOCAL CUISINE AND DINING OPTIONS

Greek cuisine is a captivating tapestry of flavors, traditions, and history, offering an exquisite fusion of Mediterranean ingredients and techniques. As a seasoned traveler with a penchant for culinary delights, allow me to guide you through the vibrant world of Athens' local cuisine and share some of the most remarkable dining experiences that will undoubtedly leave an indelible mark on your heart and taste buds.

A Journey Through the Markets: To truly immerse yourself in the culinary scene of Athens, begin your gastronomic adventure at the bustling markets. Wander through the vibrant Varvakeios Central Market, where an array of fresh produce, aromatic herbs, and traditional spices tantalize the senses. Strike up conversations with the vendors, and you may uncover family recipes passed down through generations.

Hidden Gems and Family Tavernas: Athens is a treasure trove of hidden dining gems, often found tucked away in unassuming corners of the city. Seek out charming family-run tavernas that offer a genuine taste of home-cooked meals. Be open to serendipitous encounters, and you may find yourself sharing a table with locals, exchanging stories and laughter over plates of delectable "moussaka" or "pastitsio."

The Time-Honored Ritual of Meze: Embrace the cherished Greek tradition of "meze," where meals are a delightful array of small plates meant for sharing and savoring together. Engage in the conviviality of the moment as you sample a medley of "taramasalata," "tzatziki," "spanakopita," and other meze delights. Allow the flavors to blend with the company of friends or newfound companions.

Tavernas with a View: Picture yourself in a charming taverna overlooking the Acropolis, basking in its ethereal glow as the sun sets behind the ancient citadel. The Acropolis serves as a breathtaking backdrop to your dining experience, as you relish dishes like "kleftiko," tender lamb slow-cooked to perfection, and "saganaki," a delectable fried cheese appetizer.

Farm-to-Table Delights: Delve into the farm-to-table ethos that is deeply ingrained in Greek culinary traditions. Embark on excursions to nearby farms and vineyards, where you can pluck fresh olives from the trees and taste the smoothest olive oil you've ever encountered. Savor the earthy notes of locally produced wines and the sweetness of sun-ripened fruits.

Seafood by the Aegean: As Athens is blessed with access to the Aegean Sea, indulge in an unforgettable seafood feast in the coastal neighborhoods. Discover the catch of the day prepared with expertise, from succulent grilled fish to mouthwatering "gavros," small fried fish enjoyed with a squeeze of lemon.

Sweets to Sweeten Your Soul: No culinary journey in Athens is complete without a rendezvous with the city's sweet indulgences. Treat yourself to "Loukoumades" soaked in honey and sprinkled with cinnamon, or lose yourself in the velvety layers of "galaktoboureko." And as you stroll through the picturesque Plaka district, savor the traditional "koulouri," a sesame-seed-covered bread ring, a favorite among locals and visitors alike.

A Personal Encounter: On one of my own ventures into the heart of Athens, I stumbled upon a tiny taverna that beckoned me with the tantalizing aroma of "gemista." Intrigued, I ventured in and found myself savoring the tenderest stuffed tomatoes and peppers I had ever tasted. As the owner regaled me with tales of his grandmother's recipes and the legacy of his family-run taverna, I couldn't help but feel a profound connection to the city and its culinary heritage.

Through the avenues of Athens and the embrace of its cuisine, you will come to appreciate the city's heart and soul. So, embrace the flavors, the stories, and the moments shared around the table, for in Athens, dining is not just sustenance; it is an intimate celebration of life itself.

SHOPPING IN ATHENS

As the ancient and modern converge in Athens, so does the city's shopping scene, which reflects its vibrant culture and storied past. Let me be your guide through the bustling markets, artisan boutiques, and hidden gems that make shopping in Athens an enriching and memorable experience.

The Enchanting Plaka District: Begin your shopping journey in the enchanting neighborhood of Plaka, nestled at the foot of the Acropolis. Meandering through its cobblestone streets, you'll find an array of charming shops offering traditional Greek handicrafts, such as handwoven textiles, intricate pottery, and beautiful jewelry adorned with ancient symbols. As you browse, take a moment to strike up a conversation with the artisans, who often share the stories behind their craft, passed down through generations.

Ermou Street and Kolonaki: For a taste of modernity, head to Ermou Street, Athens' main shopping thoroughfare. Here, international brands and chic boutiques line the boulevard, offering a wide range of fashion items and accessories to suit every style. If you prefer a more upscale shopping experience, venture to the elegant neighborhood of Kolonaki, where designer stores and high-end boutiques showcase the latest trends.

Emerging Greek Designers: Athens is also a hotbed of creativity and innovation, with a burgeoning community of local designers. Seek out concept stores and galleries that spotlight these emerging talents, where you can discover one-of-a-kind clothing, accessories, and home decor pieces that effortlessly blend contemporary aesthetics with traditional craftsmanship.

The Monastiraki Flea Market: A treasure trove for bargain hunters and collectors alike, the Monastiraki Flea Market is a must-visit destination. Amidst the labyrinth of stalls, you'll find a captivating assortment of antiques, vintage finds, and quirky souvenirs. Be prepared to haggle with the friendly vendors, and you may come away with unique mementos and relics that tell their own stories of Greece's rich history.

The Central Market (Varvakeios): If you're eager to immerse yourself in the vibrant local culture, a visit to Varvakeios Central Market is a must. From the early hours of the morning, this bustling market comes alive with locals seeking fresh produce, fragrant spices, and an assortment of local delicacies. As you explore the market's nooks and crannies, you'll witness the ebb and flow of daily life in Athens and discover an array of culinary delights to savor later.

A Personal Shopping Journey: On one of my own visits to Athens, I stumbled upon a small boutique tucked away in a narrow alley. The shop owner, a passionate advocate of traditional Greek craftsmanship, invited me inside and shared the story of each handcrafted item in her store. From delicate silver jewelry to intricate ceramics, I found myself drawn to the pieces that exuded the spirit of Greece's rich heritage. With each purchase, I felt a connection to the artisans and their devotion to preserving their cultural legacy.

Remember, shopping in Athens is not merely about acquiring souvenirs; it's about embracing the city's soul and carrying a piece of its essence back home with you. Whether you're exploring the bustling markets or seeking out hidden ateliers, allow yourself to be enchanted by the unique stories that each purchase holds. Through shopping, you'll discover that the heart of Athens beats not only within its historic landmarks but also within the craftsmanship and creativity of its artisans.

Chapter 9 - Beyond Athens: Discovering Hidden Archaeological Gems

*D*ear travel aficionados, if you believe Athens is the only place in Greece to dive into the past, prepare to expand your horizons! Greece is a vibrant open history book, where each page whispers tales of ancient grandeur. It's time to buckle up and embark on a thrilling journey through some of the most remarkable archaeological sites and museums beyond the bustling city of Athens.

The Ancient Theatre of Epidaurus:

From 'drama queen' back to where drama was royalty - The Ancient Theatre of Epidaurus. Constructed in the late 4th century BC, this perfectly preserved theatre is a living testament to Greek theatrical and acoustical mastery. With a semi-circular auditorium, known as the Koilon, which can accommodate up to 14,000 spectators, its acoustics still astound today. Every summer, performances of ancient Greek drama occur, allowing you to experience the magic in an authentic setting. A small caveat though, the performances may not be in English, but the sheer energy and atmosphere transcend linguistic barriers.

The Palace of Knossos in Crete:

It's time for a royal tour! The Palace of Knossos, in Crete, holds the distinction of being the largest Bronze Age archaeological site on Crete and is considered Europe's oldest city. This was where King Minos, the father of the infamous man-bull Minotaur of Greek mythology, held sway. The sprawling palace complex is a labyrinth of workrooms, living spaces, and storage rooms close to a central square. Images adorning the palace walls offer detailed glimpses into Cretan life in the late Bronze Age, letting our imaginations roam free to picture its glory days.

The Archaeological Museum of Thessaloniki:

Shifting our gaze northwards, we find ourselves in the vibrant city of Thessaloniki. Home to one of Greece's significant museums, the Archaeological Museum of Thessaloniki houses a treasure trove of artifacts from Macedonia, offering a unique insight into the region's rich history from prehistoric times to late antiquity. Highlights include the Gold of Macedon exhibition with an array of jewelry, coins, and funerary items, and the Thessaloniki Area in Prehistory exhibition, which chronicles the region's cultural evolution from the 7th to the 4th millennia BC.

Mycenae:

Venture into northeastern Peloponnese, where the ancient city of Mycenae awaits, once a major hub of Greek civilization and a formidable military stronghold. Explore the city's remains, including the famous Lion's Gate and the ancient kings' tombs.

Archaeological Site of Delos:

Situated near Mykonos, Delos is among Greece's most important archaeological sites. As per mythology, it is the birthplace of Apollo and Artemis. The entire island is a living museum, with captivating ruins that include sanctuaries, a theater, intricate mosaics, and the iconic Terrace of the Lions statues.

The Palace of the Grand Master in Rhodes:

Behold the imposing Palace of the Grand Master in Rhodes, one of the best-preserved examples of Gothic architecture in Greece. It houses a museum displaying antique furniture, Roman and Byzantine sculptures, medieval frescoes, and detailed mosaics.

Archaeological Museum of Heraklion:

Situated on Crete, this museum stands as one of Greece's greatest and Europe's most important. The museum houses artifacts from all periods of Cretan prehistory and history, spanning over 5,500 years from the Neolithic period to Roman times. Its unique Minoan collection boasts unmatched examples of Minoan art.

Akrotiri Archaeological Site in Santorini:

Finally, the Minoan Bronze Age settlement of Akrotiri in Santorini, destroyed in the Theran eruption around 1627 BC and preserved in volcanic ash, is akin to Pompeii due to the well-preserved artifacts and buildings.

Archaeological Site of Olympia:

Let's explore the birthplace of the Olympic Games, the archaeological site of Olympia in western Peloponnese. The site contains the ruins of the ancient structures, including the Temple of Zeus, which once housed the Statue of Zeus, one of the Seven Wonders of the Ancient World. The stadium where the games were held can still be seen, evoking the spirit of competition and camaraderie of ancient times.

The Sanctuary of Asklepios at Epidaurus:

Another UNESCO World Heritage site, the Sanctuary of Asklepios at Epidaurus, was a significant ancient Greek center for healing. Patients would come to this sanctuary to seek cures for their ailments. You can explore the Temple of Asklepios, the Tholos, and the Stoa of Abaton.

Meteora:

Further north, the surreal rock formations of Meteora aren't just a natural wonder but also an extraordinary example of man's desire to connect with the divine. Six monasteries are perched atop these rock pillars, constructed by monks seeking spiritual isolation and freedom from religious persecution. Each monastery is a treasure chest of Byzantine art and iconography.

Archaeological Site of Vergina:

The ancient city of Aigai, modern-day Vergina, was the first capital of the Kingdom of Macedon. Here lies the monumental palace, lavishly decorated with mosaics and painted stuccoes, and the burial ground with more than 300 tumuli, some of which date from the 11th century B.C. The most famous is the tomb of King Philip II, father of Alexander the Great.

The Archaeological Museum of Rhodes:

Located in the Medieval City of Rhodes, this museum is hosted in the former Hospital of the Knights. It contains a vast collection of artifacts from various parts of Rhodes and the neighboring islands, dating from the Neolithic age to the Early Christian times.

The Lion of Kea:

Located on the island of Kea, the Lion of Kea is a remarkable archaic sculpture carved out of the natural bedrock sometime around the 6th century BC. The smiling lion is the largest of its kind in the Cycladic islands and is shrouded in mystery as its purpose remains unknown.

The Temple of Apollo Epicurius at Bassae:

Situated in Figalia in the mountains of Arcadia, the Temple of Apollo Epicurius is a UNESCO World Heritage Site. The temple, designed by the famous architect Iktinos, is an architectural marvel, blending different architectural styles in a harmonious way.

The Archaeological Site of Delphi:

Once regarded as the center of the world in Greek mythology, Delphi is an ancient sanctuary that grew rich with the offerings of devotees. The ruins include the Temple of Apollo, the ancient theater, the stadium, and the Tholos of Delphi, with its distinct circular construction.

The Palace of Nestor:

On the hill of Epano Englianos near Pylos, the ruins of the Palace of Nestor, the best-preserved Mycenaean Greek palace, can be explored. Named after the Homeric hero Nestor, the site provides insight into the organization of a Late Bronze Age palace.

The Ancient Theatre of Dionysus in Athens:

Last but not least, the Ancient Theatre of Dionysus in Athens, the world's oldest theatre, deserves your visit. Nestled on the southern slope of the Acropolis, it was dedicated to Dionysus, the ancient Greek god of wine and drama. Here the great plays of Sophocles, Euripides, and Aristophanes were first performed.

Remember, fellow globetrotters, these historical gems' magic lies in exploring them firsthand—touching the ancient stones, feeling history hum under your fingertips. So pack your curiosity and let Greece's rich past guide you on an unforgettable journey. Stay tuned for our next chapter where we explore more hidden treasures of Greece's lesser-known islands!

CHAPTER 10 - "DIVERSE PARADISE: THE GREEK ISLANDS

*G*reece, with its enchanting islands scattered across the Aegean and Ionian Seas, offers a *paradise of diverse landscapes, rich history, and unparalleled beauty. From world-renowned destinations to hidden gems waiting to be discovered, the Greek Islands promise an unforgettable journey for every traveler.*

AN INTRODUCTION TO THE GREEK ISLANDS:

The Greek Islands consist of over 6,000 islands and islets, each with its own distinct charm and allure. These islands are grouped into several archipelagos, with the most popular ones being the Cyclades, the Dodecanese, the Ionian Islands, and the Sporades. Here's an overview of some of the most significant and captivating islands within each archipelago, listed in order of their tourist appeal:

Cyclades Archipelago:

- **Santorini:** The epitome of romance and volcanic beauty, Santorini's iconic caldera and breathtaking sunsets make it a dream destination for travelers worldwide.

- **Mykonos:** Known for its vibrant nightlife, stunning beaches, and charming whitewashed villages, Mykonos is a playground for party-goers and sun-seekers alike.

- **Naxos:** With its ancient ruins, picturesque landscapes, and long sandy beaches, Naxos offers a blend of history, culture, and relaxation.

- **Paros:** A laid-back island with traditional Cycladic architecture, Paros entices visitors with its tranquil ambiance and excellent water sports opportunities.

Dodecanese Archipelago:

- **Rhodes:** Steeped in history and dotted with medieval castles and ancient ruins, Rhodes captivates travelers with its remarkable heritage and stunning beaches.

- **Kos:** Known for its ancient healing center, Asclepeion, and beautiful sandy beaches, Kos offers a perfect blend of history and leisure.

- **Symi:** A picturesque island with neoclassical architecture and crystal-clear waters, Symi is a haven for art enthusiasts and nature lovers.

- **Patmos:** A spiritual oasis, Patmos is home to the Monastery of Saint John the Theologian and the Cave of the Apocalypse, making it an important pilgrimage site.

Ionian Islands:

- **Corfu:** A lush green paradise with Venetian architecture, Corfu boasts a rich cultural heritage and stunning beaches, attracting visitors from all walks of life.
- **Zakynthos:** Famous for its shipwreck beach and the mesmerizing Blue Caves, Zakynthos is a haven for nature enthusiasts and adventure seekers.
- **Kefalonia:** Offering dramatic landscapes, including the iconic Myrtos Beach and Melissani Cave, Kefalonia is an ideal destination for nature lovers.

Sporades Archipelago:

- **Skiathos:** Known for its vibrant nightlife and pristine sandy beaches, Skiathos is a popular choice for young travelers and party enthusiasts.
- **Skopelos:** A tranquil retreat with lush landscapes and picturesque villages, Skopelos is ideal for those seeking a peaceful escape.
- **Alonissos:** A paradise for nature lovers, Alonissos is part of the National Marine Park and is home to rare marine life and lush Mediterranean vegetation.

These are just a few of the enchanting Greek Islands that await exploration. Each island has its own distinct character, from ancient ruins and historical landmarks to idyllic beaches and vibrant nightlife. Whether you seek relaxation, adventure, cultural experiences, or simply a moment of serenity, the Greek Islands have something special to offer every traveler. In the following chapters, we will delve deeper into some of these islands, providing valuable insights and travel tips to ensure you make the most of your journey through this magical archipelago. Let's embark on an unforgettable adventure through the wonders of the Greek Islands, starting with the mesmerizing Corfu.

CORFU: THE EMERALD ISLE

Corfu, also known as Kerkyra, is an enchanting island in the Ionian Sea, known for its lush landscapes, crystal-clear waters, and energetic nightlife. As an experienced traveler, I hold a special fondness for Corfu due to its exceptional beauty and the hospitality of its people.

Highlights of Corfu

My first visit to Corfu is etched in my memory. The must-visit sites include the Old Fortress in Corfu Town, a Venetian fortress with a rich history, providing a glimpse into the island's varied cultural influences. Wandering through the Liston in Corfu Town offers a unique charm. This Parisian-style arcade with numerous cafes and restaurants is a perfect spot to relax and observe the island's vibrant life. The panoramic view of the Old Town, the Ionian Sea, and distant mountains from the New Fortress is absolutely breathtaking and gives a profound sense of the island's layout. A boat trip to the Paxos and Antipaxos islands is another highlight. Offering an opportunity to swim in the incredibly clear turquoise waters, these islands are a slice of paradise. For a more adventurous experience, exploring the diverse underwater world of Corfu through scuba diving is an unforgettable encounter with the local marine life.

Paleokastritsa and Achillion Palace

Perhaps, Corfu is most famous for Paleokastritsa, a place of diverse landscapes, where you can find green hills, crystal-clear azure waters, and picturesque small bays. The monastery of Paleokastritsa, standing on a hill, offers captivating views over the bays and is worth a visit.

The Achillion Palace, another iconic spot, was built for Empress Elizabeth of Austria and later owned by Kaiser Wilhelm II of Germany. The palace, with its beautiful gardens, neoclassical statues, and stunning views of Corfu, speaks volumes about the history and the personalities that influenced Corfu during their reign.

Let me share a personal anecdote. I remember wandering through the narrow streets of Corfu Old Town. With no rush and no crowds, I was free to immerse myself in the historic beauty of the town, experiencing the local lifestyle and relishing traditional Corfiot cuisine. It was one of the most charming moments of my life, deepening my connection to the Greek islands.

As a word of advice, if you're planning to visit Corfu during peak season, I suggest booking your excursions and activities in advance to secure your spot. And remember, always respect the natural environment, leaving it as pristine as you found it for others to enjoy.

KERKYRA, CORFU

As the ferry approaches the crescent-shaped island of Santorini, one is instantly captivated by the sight of its iconic whitewashed buildings perched precariously on the cliffs, overlooking the azure waters of the Aegean Sea. Renowned as one of the most romantic and picturesque destinations in the world, Santorini is a jewel that never fails to leave travelers spellbound.

SANTORINI

A Tale of Myth and Volcanoes: Legend has it that Santorini is the remnants of the lost city of Atlantis, which was submerged beneath the sea after a catastrophic volcanic eruption. While the story may be a mythical tale, the island's volcanic history is very real. The massive volcanic eruption that occurred around 1600 BCE shaped the island's unique caldera, creating the awe-inspiring landscape we see today.

Exploring the Caldera and Beyond: The caldera, a vast crater formed by the volcanic eruption, is the heart of Santorini's allure. Fira and Oia, two of the island's most picturesque towns, cling to the caldera cliffs, offering breathtaking panoramic views and unforgettable sunsets. Strolling through the narrow cobblestone streets, visitors can immerse themselves in the Cycladic architecture and discover charming boutiques, art galleries, and quaint cafes.

Beyond the caldera, Santorini unveils its diverse character. The island's eastern coast boasts stunning black sand beaches, such as Kamari and Perissa, formed by the volcanic activity. The southern part of the island features the captivating Red Beach, known for its distinctive red cliffs and pebbles. Additionally, the ancient Minoan site of Akrotiri offers a glimpse into the island's rich history, with well-preserved ruins of a prehistoric settlement.

Exquisite Culinary Delights: A visit to Santorini is an opportunity to savor a gastronomic journey like no other. The island's volcanic soil and unique microclimate yield exceptional produce and wines. Be sure to try the famous cherry tomatoes, white eggplants, and fava beans, all grown in Santorini's fertile volcanic soil. For wine enthusiasts, a wine tour of the island's vineyards is a must, with the chance to taste distinctive Assyrtiko wines and the sweet Vinsanto.

The Warm Embrace of Hospitality: The warmth and hospitality of the people of Santorini create an unforgettable experience for visitors. Engaging with the locals, listening to their stories, and learning about their customs enriches the journey beyond just the stunning landscapes.

Romance and Memories: It is no wonder that Santorini has become a beloved destination for couples seeking an idyllic getaway. The sunsets, the intimate candlelit dinners, and the charming accommodations carved into the cliffs all contribute to an atmosphere of enchanting romance.

Practical Tips for Santorini Travel:

- **Best Time to Visit:** While Santorini can be enjoyed throughout the year, the best time to visit is during the shoulder seasons of spring (April to June) and autumn (September to October) when the weather is pleasant, and the crowds are thinner.

- **Accommodations:** From luxury boutique hotels to traditional cave houses, Santorini offers a variety of accommodations to suit every traveler's preferences. It is advisable to book well in advance, especially for stays in Oia and Fira.

- **Transportation:** While the island has an efficient local bus system, renting a car or ATV provides the freedom to explore at your own pace, especially if you plan to visit remote beaches and archaeological sites.

- **Sunset Viewing Spots:** For the best sunset experience, head to Oia's Byzantine Castle Ruins or Amoudi Bay. Remember to arrive early to secure a good spot.

- **Dining Recommendations:** Embrace the local culinary scene by trying traditional dishes like moussaka, souvlaki, and baklava. Seek out local tavernas for an authentic taste of Santorinian cuisine.

Santorini's allure lies not only in its stunning vistas and captivating landscapes but also in the way it enchants travelers' hearts. From sun-kissed beaches and charming villages to delectable cuisine and genuine hospitality, Santorini is a destination that will forever hold a special place in the memories of those fortunate enough to experience its magic. As you embark on your Santorini adventure, allow yourself to be swept away by the island's enchanting allure and create memories that will last a lifetime.

EXPLORING SANTORINI: ISLAND HIGHLIGHTS

Santorini, with its breathtaking landscapes and captivating allure, offers a plethora of activities to delight every type of traveler. Whether you seek adventure, relaxation, or cultural exploration, this enchanting island has something special in store for you.

1. Witness Mesmerizing Sunsets: As the day draws to a close, make your way to Oia or Amoudi Bay to experience one of the most iconic sunsets in the world. The sky becomes a canvas of vibrant hues, creating an enchanting spectacle that leaves an indelible mark on your heart.

2. Discover Historic Sites: Explore the ancient ruins of Akrotiri, known as the "Minoan Pompeii," where a prehistoric civilization was preserved beneath volcanic ash. Delve into the island's rich past and unearth the mysteries of this well-preserved archaeological site.

3. Beach Bliss: Santorini's beaches are diverse and unique. Unwind on the striking Red Beach, with its crimson cliffs and clear waters, or visit the volcanic black sand beaches of Kamari and Perissa. For a quieter experience, seek out the less-frequented Vlychada Beach, known for its lunar-like landscape.

4. Volcanic Excursion: Embark on a boat tour to Nea Kameni, the volcanic islet within the caldera, and hike up to the summit of the active volcano. Witnessing the awe-inspiring views of the caldera from this vantage point is an experience unlike any other.

5. Wine Tasting Journey: Santorini's volcanic soil produces unique wines, and a wine tour is a delightful way to sample the island's distinctive flavors. Visit local wineries, learn about the island's winemaking traditions, and indulge in tastings of the famous Assyrtiko and Vinsanto wines.

6. Exploring the Villages: Wander through the charming villages of Oia, Fira, and Imerovigli, each offering its own unique charm and beauty. Lose yourself in the labyrinthine streets, adorned with bougainvillea and blue-domed churches.

7. Cruise to the Hot Springs: Take a boat tour to the Palea Kameni islet to immerse yourself in the therapeutic waters of the hot springs, known for their rejuvenating properties. Enjoy a swim in the warm, sulfur-rich waters and bask in the stunning surroundings.

8. Adventures on the Water: For water enthusiasts, Santorini offers a myriad of activities, from snorkeling and scuba diving to stand-up paddleboarding. Discover the vibrant marine life and underwater caves that dot the island's coastline.

9. Local Cuisine Delights: Indulge in the delectable offerings of Santorini's gastronomic scene. Savor traditional Greek dishes, including fresh seafood, fava, and tomatokeftedes, in quaint tavernas overlooking the sea.

10. Romantic Experiences: Santorini is renowned as a romantic haven, and there's no shortage of intimate experiences to share with your loved one. Take a private sailing cruise, enjoy a candlelit dinner with the caldera as your backdrop, or simply revel in the beauty of your surroundings hand in hand.

Remember, the essence of Santorini lies not only in ticking off attractions but in embracing the island's unique ambiance and creating cherished memories. Allow yourself to wander off the beaten path, interact with locals, and be open to unexpected adventures that may come your way. Santorini is a destination that beckons with its beauty and captivates with its charm, making every moment a treasured experience. Whether you're a seasoned traveler or a first-time visitor, this magical island will leave you forever enchanted.

BEACHES OF SANTORINI: WHERE PARADISE MEETS THE AEGEAN

Santorini's beaches are like jewels scattered along its coastline, each radiating its own unique charm. From the iconic Red Beach to hidden coves, the island offers a diverse array of coastal havens for beach lovers to indulge in sun-soaked relaxation and water-based adventures.

1. Red Beach (Kokkini Paralia): Nestled at the foot of dramatic red cliffs, the Red Beach stands as a testament to the island's volcanic origins. The striking contrast between the red-hued volcanic sands and the turquoise waters of the Aegean Sea creates an otherworldly ambiance that is simply mesmerizing. Arrive early to secure a good spot, as this beach can get crowded during peak hours.

2. Kamari Beach: Known for its impressive stretch of black volcanic sand, Kamari Beach offers a lively and vibrant atmosphere. Here, you can find an abundance of beachfront cafes, tavernas, and water sports facilities. It's an ideal spot for families and those seeking a mix of relaxation and beachside entertainment.

3. Perissa Beach: Adjacent to Kamari Beach, Perissa boasts the same captivating black sands and a laid-back vibe. The eastern end of the beach is dominated by the magnificent Mesa Vouno rock, adding a unique backdrop to your beach day. Take advantage of the water sports activities or simply unwind under the umbrellas, indulging in the serene beauty of the surroundings.

4. Vlychada Beach: A hidden gem on the southern coast, Vlychada Beach beckons with its lunar-like landscape. The unique rock formations and white cliffs give the beach an otherworldly charm. For a touch of luxury, you can relax at the elegant Vlychada Beach Club, offering sunbeds, umbrellas, and excellent dining options.

5. White Beach (Aspri Paralia): Accessible only by boat or on foot from Red Beach, the White Beach rewards those who venture to reach its shores. The pristine pebbles and clear waters create an idyllic setting for a more secluded beach experience. The surrounding cliffs provide shade during the day, making it a perfect spot to unwind in tranquility.

6. Agios Georgios (Black Beach): Located near Perivolos, Agios Georgios Beach is a quieter alternative to the bustling Kamari and Perissa beaches. Relax under the sun on the soft black sands, and treat yourself to fresh seafood at the traditional tavernas lining the shore.

7. Cape Columbo Beach: For those seeking solitude and untouched nature, Cape Columbo Beach is a secluded retreat on the northeastern coast. The beach is renowned for its dark volcanic sands and deep blue waters, surrounded by a rugged landscape that adds an air of mystique to the experience.

8. Exo Gialos Beach: Situated near Fira, Exo Gialos offers a serene and less touristy atmosphere. The beach is covered in small pebbles and offers a quiet escape where you can unwind and rejuvenate away from the crowds.

Remember to bring plenty of water, sunscreen, and beach essentials as amenities can vary between beaches. Each beach presents its own allure, and whether you're seeking relaxation, exploration, or adventure, Santorini's coastline promises an unforgettable experience that will stay with you long after you leave its shores.

WINDMILLS OF MYKONOS

EXPLORING MYKONOS: THE ISLAND OF THE WINDS

Mykonos, fondly referred to as the "Island of the Winds," is a beacon of the Cyclades, a grouping of Greek islands in the Aegean Sea. This idyllic destination is lauded for its thrilling nightlife, breathtaking beaches, and the quintessential windmills that paint a picture of traditional Greek island life.

Mykonos' reputation as a hotspot for partygoers from across the globe precedes it. As the sun sets, the island springs to life with pulsating music and lively crowds thronging beachside bars and elegant nightclubs. Paradise Beach and Super Paradise Beach are especially known for their day-to-night parties.

Yet there's more to Mykonos than just its energetic nightlife. The island is also a haven of tranquility and tradition. Its charm lies in the balance between the high-spirited parties and the serene, picturesque corners where you can revel in the beauty of the Aegean Sea at your own pace.

Take a leisurely stroll through the labyrinthine streets of Mykonos Town, or as the locals call it, 'Chora'. Here, narrow marble-paved alleys twist and turn between whitewashed houses adorned with colorful doors and windows, vibrant bougainvillea cascading down their facades. This maze-like design, originally intended to confuse marauding pirates, now invites visitors to lose themselves in the timeless allure of Mykonian architecture.

No visit to Mykonos is complete without spending an evening in Little Venice. Here, rows of quaint, old houses line the waterfront, their balconies overhanging the sea. I vividly remember an evening spent in one of the seaside tavernas, feasting on 'kopanisti' (peppery cheese) and fresh seafood, while the setting sun painted the sky with brilliant streaks of orange and purple.

The island's iconic windmills, known as 'Kato Mili', are another must-visit. Standing on a hill overlooking Mykonos Town, these 16th-century windmills offer panoramic views of the town and the sea beyond. I found it to be the perfect spot to enjoy the sunset, with the windmills silhouetted against the amber sky, an image that will stay with me forever.

On the historical front, the nearby island of Delos offers a unique opportunity to delve into Greek mythology. Known as the mythological birthplace of Apollo and Artemis, Delos boasts an array of well-preserved ancient ruins that will satisfy the history buff in you. It's just a short boat ride from Mykonos, and I recommend dedicating a day to exploring this UNESCO World Heritage site.

For beach lovers, Mykonos offers a variety of options, each with its unique charm. From the family-friendly Ornos Beach to the tranquil Agios Ioannis Beach, and the vibrant Paradise Beach, you're spoiled for choice. One of my personal favorites is Elia Beach, the longest sandy beach on Mykonos, offering a peaceful respite from the bustling town.

In Mykonos, every experience leaves a lingering impression, and every memory feels like a treasured keepsake. Whether you're a party enthusiast, a history aficionado, a food lover, or a leisure seeker, Mykonos has something to captivate you. Let this charming island surprise and enchant you with its contrasts and timeless beauty.

BLUE CAVES ON ZAKYNTHOS ISLAND

Zakynthos: The Flower of the East

Zakynthos, or Zante as it's often called, is a captivating island of the Ionian Sea, known for its verdant landscapes, crystalline waters, and vibrant nightlife. As a seasoned traveler, I hold a particular affection for Zakynthos due to its exceptional beauty and the hospitality of its people.

Highlights of Zakynthos

My first visit to Zakynthos is etched in my memory. One of the must-visit sites is the Byzantine Museum in Zakynthos Town, which houses an impressive collection of artwork and religious icons, providing a glimpse into the island's rich history.

In contrast, wandering through the village of Bochali, at the top of the hill overlooking Zakynthos Town, offers a different kind of thrill. The panoramic view of the town, the Ionian Sea, and the distant mainland is breathtaking and gives you a profound sense of the island's layout.

A boat trip to the Keri Caves is another highlight, offering an opportunity to swim in the unbelievably clear blue waters. But for a more adventurous experience, try scuba diving in these caves – it's a truly unforgettable encounter with the local marine life.

Blue Caves and Shipwreck Beach

Zakynthos is perhaps most famous for its Shipwreck Beach (Navagio Beach), where the wreck of a smuggler's ship lies in the middle of a sandy cove, surrounded by towering cliffs. To fully appreciate the grandeur of this sight, I recommend viewing it from both the sea and the cliff-top platform. The journey to the platform is quite an adventure in itself!

The Blue Caves, another iconic natural attraction, is best visited in the morning when the light is perfect for highlighting the water's stunning blue hue. The caves are accessible only by boat, which adds an exciting element of exploration to the experience.

Allow me to share a personal anecdote. I remember once hiring a small private boat to explore the Blue Caves. With no rush and no crowds, I was free to immerse myself in the serene beauty of the caves at my own pace. It was one of the most peaceful moments of my life, amplifying my deep connection to the Greek islands.

In the spirit of providing useful advice, let me suggest that if you're planning to visit Zakynthos during peak season, book your boat trips in advance to secure a place. And remember, always respect the natural environment, leaving it as pristine as you found it for others to enjoy.

DISCOVERING CRETE:
THE CRADLE OF MINOAN CIVILIZATION

Crete, the largest of the Greek islands and the fifth largest in the Mediterranean, has been a crossroad of civilizations for millennia. Nestled between the Aegean and Libyan seas, the island is the birthplace of the Minoans, Europe's first advanced civilization. But more than its size and history, Crete is an island of mesmerizing beauty, cultural depth, and hospitable warmth that truly sets it apart.

Stepping onto the island is like entering a vibrant, open-air museum. The rich past reverberates through the Minoan palaces of Knossos and Phaistos, the Venetian fortresses like the majestic Koules Fortress in Heraklion, the quaint monasteries nestled amidst mountains, and the Old Towns of Rethymnon and Chania, where intricate Ottoman and Venetian architecture is beautifully preserved.

Crete's nature is as multifaceted as its history. The rugged, mountainous interior, dominated by the towering Mount Ida and the awe-inspiring Samaria Gorge, stands in stark contrast with the idyllic beaches framing the island, such as Elafonissi with its distinctive pink sand, the exotic palm forest of Vai, and the lagoon of Balos. A unique network of hiking trails makes Crete a paradise for those who want to explore its captivating landscapes.

THE PALACE OF KNOSSOS IN CRETE

What truly adds life to these historic sites and stunning landscapes is the remarkable Cretan culture. Cretans, known for their exceptional hospitality, maintain strong ties with their past. The island's traditional music, featuring the soulful sounds of the Cretan lyra and the laouto, the traditional dances, and age-old customs and festivals, all contribute to the island's cultural tapestry.

Gastronomy is another area where Crete shines. The Cretan diet, considered one of the healthiest in the world, offers a unique culinary experience. Local cheeses like mizithra and graviera, the renowned Cretan olive oil, dakos (a bread-rusk salad), gamopilafo (Cretan risotto), and raki, the local spirit, are just a few examples of the island's gastronomic wealth.

All in all, Crete is not just a destination; it's an experience. The harmonious blend of historic grandeur, stunning natural beauty, rich cultural traditions, and mouth-watering cuisine, combined with the warm hospitality of its people, makes this island a unique destination for those seeking to understand the essence of Greece. From its enchanting myths to its vibrant present, Crete stands as a testament to the enduring charm of Greek civilization.

My first time setting foot in Crete, I felt as if I was entering a world where the ancient past and the lively present blend seamlessly. Crete's proud history is marked by the Minoan Civilization, which was Europe's first advanced civilization dating back to 2700-1420 BC. The archaeological sites of Knossos, Phaistos, and Malia, with their intricate palaces and mythological connotations, provide a glimpse into this prosperous era. If you've heard the myth of the Minotaur, you'll find it thrilling to explore Knossos, the legendary labyrinth where the beast was said to have been held.

Venture further inland, and you'll discover Crete's rugged mountainous landscapes, punctuated by idyllic villages where life unfolds at a leisurely pace. The Samaria Gorge in the White Mountains, one of the longest gorges in Europe, is a paradise for hiking enthusiasts. Trekking through the gorge on a cool spring morning, with the scent of wild herbs filling the air, remains one of my most cherished experiences.

Crete is also famous for its pristine beaches. On the southern coast, you'll find the exotic Elafonisi with its pink-tinted sand, while to the west, the lagoon of Balos astounds with its turquoise waters. But my personal favorite is the secluded Seitan Limania - a narrow cove tucked away between towering cliffs. Despite the somewhat challenging path to get there, the sight that greeted me was beyond worth it - azure waters enveloped in a breathtaking rock formation.

Let's not forget the charming harbor towns of Chania and Rethymno. Strolling along the narrow streets of their old towns, one can admire Venetian-era mansions, Byzantine monasteries, and Ottoman mosques, testaments to the island's layered history. I still remember the joy of savoring a 'bougatsa' (a local cream-filled pastry) at a traditional café in Chania's Old Venetian Harbour, as I watched the sun slowly set over the lighthouse.

However, what sets Crete apart is its rich culinary tradition. With a focus on locally sourced ingredients and simple yet flavorful recipes, Cretan cuisine is a pivotal component of the Mediterranean diet. I have fond memories of being welcomed into a 'taverna' in a small mountain village, where the host served us 'dakos' (rusks topped with tomatoes and mizithra cheese), freshly baked bread, and other homemade delicacies, paired with robust local wine.

Crete is more than just an island. It is a living, breathing museum of cultural heritage, a nature lover's dream, and a foodie's paradise. Above all, it is the epitome of Greek 'philoxenia' - the love of strangers, which you will experience in every interaction with the warm and hospitable Cretans. Discover Crete, delve into its enchanting past, and immerse yourself in its vibrant present. It's a journey you won't forget.

RHODES: THE ISLAND OF THE KNIGHTS
RODI MAP

Nestled at the southeastern edge of the Aegean Sea, Rhodes - the largest of the Dodecanese islands - beckons travelers with its vibrant blend of history, culture, and natural beauty. Named the Island of the Knights for its historical association with the Knights Hospitaller during the Middle Ages, Rhodes stands as a testament to a past that's layered with civilizations, from ancient Greeks and Romans to Byzantines, Knights, and Ottomans.

Begin your journey in the Old Town of Rhodes, a UNESCO World Heritage site that's encased within a medieval wall. Within these formidable fortifications, you'll discover a time capsule that harks back to the age of knights. Wander through the cobblestone Street of the Knights, one of the best-preserved medieval streets in Europe, leading to the grandeur of the Palace of the Grand Master. Once the Knights Hospitaller's headquarters, today this imposing castle serves as a museum showcasing captivating mosaics and medieval artifacts.

But Rhodes is more than its knightly past. Venture into the New Town, where Italian architecture reflects the island's occupation during the early 20th century. The Modern Art Museum, the Aquarium, and Mandraki Harbor, with its iconic deer statues and medieval windmills, offer a contrasting experience to the Old Town.

Just an hour's drive from the city, you'll find the village of Lindos, renowned for its ancient acropolis, whitewashed houses, and beautiful bay. It's a great spot to appreciate Rhodes' ancient history while enjoying panoramic views of the coastline.

Nature enthusiasts will love the Valley of Petaloudes (Butterfly Valley), a unique nature reserve filled with Jersey Tiger Moths between June and September. Additionally, the island's interior is crisscrossed with walking trails leading to verdant forests, serene lakes, and the stunning Seven Springs gorge.

Rhodes' diverse coastline offers a beach for every preference, from the bustling Faliraki and the windsurfing haven of Prasonisi to the more tranquil waters of Haraki or the unique landscape of Anthony Quinn Bay.

LESVOS

While Santorini, Mykonos, Rhodes and Crete capture much of the limelight, the Greek archipelago is made up of over 6,000 islands and islets, each with its own unique allure. As an avid traveler, I can attest that some of the most rewarding Greek island experiences can be found off the beaten path. Here are a few other gems that are truly worth exploring.

Lesbos (Lesvos): This large island in the northeastern Aegean is renowned for its dense forests, hot springs, and an ancient petrified forest declared a UNESCO Geopark. It's also the birthplace of famous ancient poets Sappho and Alcaeus. The medieval castle in Mytilene, the capital, and the picturesque town of Molyvos are worth a visit. I recall a memorable afternoon spent sipping locally produced ouzo in one of the traditional distilleries in Plomari.

Paros: Located in the heart of the Cyclades, Paros offers a mix of vibrant beach life, traditional villages, and significant historical sites. The Church of 100 Doors (Panagia Ekatontapiliani), one of the oldest Christian churches in Greece, resides here. From the white marble quarries of Marathi to the breathtaking views of the Aegean from Kolympethres beach, Paros never ceases to surprise and delight.

Naxos: As the largest and greenest island in the Cyclades, Naxos is known for its rich history, towering mountain peaks, and lush valleys. From the iconic Portara (the doorway to an unfinished temple of Apollo) near Naxos town, to the stunning mountain village of Apeiranthos with its unique marble-paved streets, the island is filled with enchanting locations. The local 'kitron' liqueur is a must-try.

Hydra: Close to Athens, Hydra stands out for its preserved elegance and unique architecture. Vehicles are notably absent here, making it a haven of tranquility. The island's steep alleys, 18th-century mansions, and the artists' workshops are all within walking distance from Hydra's port. The memory of a donkey ride through Hydra's cobblestone streets is still vivid in my mind.

Ithaca: Known as the home of Odysseus from Homer's Odyssey, Ithaca is an island steeped in mythology. The island is a collage of delightful small beaches, lush green landscapes, and picturesque bays. A trip to the Archaeological Museum of Ithaca and a stroll through the streets of Vathy, the island's main town, offer an insight into the island's rich history and legends.

Exploring these less frequented islands provides not only a sense of adventure but also an opportunity to delve deeper into the fabric of Greek island life. Each island has its own spirit, an embodiment of Greece's timeless beauty, vibrant culture, and renowned hospitality.

Chapter 11 - Mainland Destinations
Venturing Deeper into Greece's Heartland

*T*he enchanting allure of Greece extends far beyond the sandy beaches and blue waters of its famous islands. The mainland, often overshadowed by these seaside paradises, is a trove of historic sites, vibrant cities, captivating landscapes, and local traditions that offer rich, immersive experiences. This chapter will guide you through an exploration of the mainland's most compelling destinations, uncovering the layers of Greek history, culture, and natural beauty.

TEMPLE OF APOLLO (DELPHI)

Delphi: The Navel of the Ancient World

Situated on the slopes of Mount Parnassus, Delphi was considered by the ancients as the center, or 'navel', of the world. It was here that the famed Oracle of Delphi, located within the majestic Temple of Apollo, imparted cryptic prophecies to those seeking guidance, from humble individuals to great kings. Today, the archaeological site is a testament to its historic grandeur, with the theater and stadium offering breathtaking views over the valley below. Don't forget to visit the nearby museum housing a collection of artifacts discovered in Delphi, including the magnificent bronze Charioteer.

Meteora and Kalambaka: Where Heaven Meets Earth

Next, let's head north to central Greece, where the awe-inspiring Meteora awaits. The sight of monasteries perched atop towering sandstone pillars is an image that you won't soon forget. This UNESCO World Heritage Site was once a refuge for Orthodox monks seeking solitude and communion with the divine. Today, a visit to Meteora offers an uplifting experience that transcends religion. Not far from Meteora lies Kalambaka, a town that blends traditional charm with modern comforts. It's the perfect base for exploring Meteora, with opportunities for rock-climbing, hiking, or simply savoring local cuisine after a day of exploration.

Thessaloniki: The Vibrant Cultural Hub

Thessaloniki, Greece's second-largest city, is a vibrant cosmopolitan hub teeming with life, history, and culture. The city's rich past is reflected in its various architectural styles, from Roman, Byzantine, and Ottoman influences to modern structures. Take a walk along the bustling Aristotelous Square, visit the iconic White Tower, and let yourself be enchanted by the Byzantine Walls' panoramic views. Thessaloniki is also a gastronomic paradise. Its markets brim with fresh, local produce, and you can indulge in mouthwatering local specialties, such as Bougatsa and Souvlaki, in its many tavernas.

Nafplio and the Peloponnese: A Journey into the Past

Nafplio, often cited as one of Greece's prettiest towns, is a gem on the Peloponnese peninsula. Its picturesque, Venetian-style old town is a joy to explore, with narrow streets lined with neoclassical mansions and fortified by the Palamidi Castle that overlooks the town from a nearby hill. Beyond Nafplio, the Peloponnese offers a treasure trove of ancient sites, including the imposing theatre at Epidaurus and the legendary palace of Mycenae, home to the mythical King Agamemnon.

Ioannina: The Lakefront Jewel

Ioannina, a stunning city by the lake, greets its visitors with an inviting blend of natural beauty, rich history, and a lively modern culture. The city is a gateway to the less-explored Epirus region, home to the ancient theater of Dodona and the enchanting stone villages of Zagori.

Mount Olympus and Lake Plastira: The Enchanting North

Venture north to explore the mythical Mount Olympus, home of the ancient Greek gods, and experience the tranquility of Lake Plastira, a haven for nature lovers. These destinations, combined with the unique Drach Cave in Macedonia, show a different, equally compelling, side of Greece.

The Rugged Beauty of Mani

Finally, we delve into the rugged beauty of Mani, a region in the southern Peloponnese, known for its imposing tower houses and pristine, wild landscapes. Its scenic coastal villages, such as Gythio and Kardamyli, offer a serene and genuine Greek experience.

Thessaly: A Land of Myths and Natural Splendors

Moving eastwards, we arrive in Thessaly, a region teeming with natural beauty and mythological lore. It is here that the legendary battle between the Titans and the Olympian gods took place. The region is also home to the mesmerizing Lake Plastira, an idyllic spot perfect for hiking, mountain biking, or simply enjoying a picnic by the water. Nearby, the town of Meteora, with its monasteries perched atop towering cliffs, offers a unique blend of natural beauty and spiritual heritage.

The Evocative Epirus: From the Oracle of Dodona to Zagori Villages

Lastly, we venture to the region of Epirus, home to one of the most ancient oracle sites in Greece, Dodona. Here, the whispering oak trees were believed to reveal the gods' will. The region is also known for its Zagori villages, a network of 46 stone-built settlements nestled in the Pindus mountains. These villages are a testament to the architectural and cultural traditions of Epirus and serve as an excellent base for exploring the breathtaking Vikos Gorge.

In each corner of mainland Greece, there's a story to tell, a sight to behold, and a unique experience to embrace. From ancient oracle sites and spiritual monasteries to enchanting stone villages and splendid natural wonders, these additional destinations further enrich your Greek journey, offering new perspectives and memorable encounters.

GYROS IN A PITA BREAD

Chapter 12: Greek Cuisine - A Journey of Flavor

*G*reece's sun-soaked landscapes are not only stunning to look at but also fertile grounds for an abundance of fresh, flavorful ingredients that make Greek cuisine one of the most beloved around the world. The Greek table is a celebration of life itself - vibrant, fragrant, and steeped in a history as rich as the land from which it springs. Let's embark on a culinary journey that is sure to satisfy our senses and soul, exploring the country's gastronomic traditions and iconic dishes.

Introduction to Greek Food: More Than Just a Meal

The philosophy of Greek cuisine can be encapsulated in three words: fresh, simple, and flavorful. From the glistening olives harvested under the Mediterranean sun to the hand-made phyllo pastries that melt in your mouth, every dish is a testament to the Greeks' deep-rooted respect for the land and its bounty. Greek meals are not just about sustenance but an experience that fosters camaraderie, discussion, and enjoyment. Dining is a social event, often stretching out over hours, as meze (small dishes) make their way onto the table, glasses clink, and laughter floats on the warm evening air.

Famous Greek dishes such as Moussaka, Souvlaki, and Tzatziki are just the beginning. Each region of Greece has its unique specialties, reflecting the area's local products and historical influences. An exploration of Greek food is akin to a voyage around the country, from the hearty meat dishes of the mountainous regions to the vegetable and seafood-rich diet of the islands.

Remember, while restaurants and tavernas offer a great chance to sample Greek cuisine, consider visiting local markets too. Here, amidst the colorful bustle, you can immerse yourself in the daily life of Greeks, exploring fresh fruits, vegetables, cheeses, olives, and other staples of Greek cuisine. And if you have a chance, join a local cooking class. There's nothing quite like the satisfaction of preparing your Greek meal, a memory you'll treasure and a skill you'll take home.

On this gastronomic journey, we'll delve into iconic dishes, regional specialties, sweet delicacies, and the famed Greek beverages, offering you a comprehensive guide to Greek cuisine. So, loosen your belt and prepare your taste buds for an epicurean adventure unlike any other.

Traditional Dishes to Try: A Symphony of Flavors

Embarking on the journey of Greek cuisine is like setting sail on an emerald sea brimming with hidden treasures, each dish offering a tantalizing glimpse into the soul of this vibrant country. Here, I'll share with you some of my most cherished culinary discoveries, transporting you from the bustling tavernas of Athens to the tranquil olive groves of Crete.

Moussaka

Arguably the superstar of Greek cuisine, Moussaka is a heavenly layering of juicy, seasoned minced meat, slices of aubergine and potato, all topped with a lusciously creamy béchamel sauce and then baked to golden perfection. I remember the first time I had Moussaka at a local taverna in Athens, the host, a cheerful man named Yannis, served me a generous portion, and with the first bite, I felt like I was part of a Greek family's Sunday lunch.

Souvlaki and Gyros

The streets of Thessaloniki echo with the sizzling sounds of Souvlaki and Gyros. Skewered pieces of marinated pork (or chicken, lamb, beef) are grilled to perfection and served either on a pita bread with tzatziki, tomatoes, onions, and a sprinkling of paprika, or on the skewer, with a side of bread. Gyros, similarly, are made with meat cooked on a vertical rotisserie, typically served wrapped in a flatbread. Don't be shy to ask for extra tzatziki – its cool, tangy flavor is a delight in every bite!

Dolmades

Strolling through a local market in Nafplio, I was captivated by the sight of an elderly woman meticulously wrapping grape leaves around a filling of rice and herbs. These are Dolmades, an authentic Greek delight. Savour each one, as every bite narrates a tale of tradition and patience.

Spanakopita

Fresh, crispy phyllo pastry encases a heart of spinach, feta cheese, onions, and seasonings, making Spanakopita a must-try. I fondly remember sitting in a small cafe in Delphi, the crisp mountain air filled with the aroma of fresh Spanakopita, a perfect companion to the breathtaking view of the ancient ruins.

Taramasalata

A creamy blend of cured fish roe, olive oil, lemon juice, and bread or potatoes, Taramasalata is a delectable dip that graces every Greek table. Its unique, tangy flavor will have you dipping and spreading with gusto.

The beauty of Greek cuisine is its diversity, its celebration of local produce, and its embodiment of Greek philosophies of life. Each dish sings its song of flavors, and as travelers, we have the privilege of listening and tasting this edible history and culture. So, grab a fork (or a piece of bread), and prepare for a culinary journey that not only satisfies your hunger but also feeds your soul.

No culinary journey to Greece would be complete without indulging in the country's aromatic and potent beverages. Just as the cerulean Aegean Sea laps against a myriad of Greek islands, so too does the Greek beverage culture overflow with depth and diversity. Allow me to guide you through the intoxicating labyrinth of Greek drinks, recalling memories of sunsets over the Santorini caldera and spirited discussions in bustling Athenian kafeneia.

Ouzo

An anise-flavored aperitif, Ouzo is as quintessentially Greek as the iconic white-washed houses of Mykonos. The drink, usually served with a platter of meze, imparts a distinctive sweet, yet slightly bitter, licorice taste that's both refreshing and revivifying. I remember my first sip of Ouzo in a seaside taverna in Crete, where the cool evening breeze mingled with the warm spirit of local revelers.

Retsina

A distinctive Greek white or rosé wine, Retsina carries the aroma and flavor of pine resin – a characteristic that goes back to ancient wine-making traditions. Retsina may be an acquired taste, but once you've taken a liking to it, sipping this wine on a balmy Greek evening can become a cherished memory. It surely has for me.

Tsipouro and Tsikoudia

Potent and fiery, Tsipouro and its Cretan cousin Tsikoudia, often called Raki, are strong spirits that form an integral part of local Greek tradition. The ritual of enjoying these drinks is as important as the drinks themselves. A shot of Tsipouro, accompanied by laughter and lively conversation, has made many of my Greek nights unforgettable.

Metaxa

A blend of brandy and wine, Metaxa holds an allure that's hard to resist. With its velvety smoothness and floral notes, Metaxa brings an end to a meal in a manner that only a Greek symposium might have rivaled.

Greek Coffee

And then, there's Greek coffee – thick, strong, and traditionally brewed in a small pot known as a "briki." Coffee in Greece is not just a beverage, but a ritual, a break from the daily grind, and an opportunity for conversation. There are few better pleasures than enjoying this rich, frothy coffee while gazing out at the shimmering Aegean.

Each sip of these traditional Greek drinks narrates a tale – of ancient traditions, convivial celebrations, or quiet contemplation. As you wander through the whitewashed streets or hike along rugged island trails, let these beverages quench your thirst and invigorate your Greek adventure. As they say in Greece, "Yamas!" – "To our health!"

Chapter 13: Activities and Adventures - Embracing the Greek Spirit

*U*nfolding like a grand epic, Greece offers far more than meets the eye. Each corner of this captivating country brims with potential for exploration and adventure, thus inviting travelers to truly immerse themselves in the Greek way of life. The best way to experience Greece is not through a bus window or from a sun lounger, but by actively engaging with the landscape, the culture, and the people.

From hiking the rugged mountain paths to dancing the night away at a traditional Greek panigyri, the Greek spirit of "kefi" – joy, enthusiasm, passion – is infectious. This chapter aims to introduce you to some of the thrilling activities and adventures you can undertake while exploring Greece. Whether you are an adrenaline junkie, a nature lover, a history buff, or a social butterfly, Greece has something for everyone.

With this sentiment in mind, let us lace up our boots and set off on the first of these adventures: hiking and trekking in Greece's diverse landscapes.

Gods and Heroes: Hiking and Trekking

The rugged Greek landscapes, crisscrossed with ancient paths, offer some of the most stunning hiking and trekking opportunities in the world. From the hallowed slopes of Mount Olympus to the wild, untamed beauty of the Samaria Gorge in Crete, Greece has trails that appeal to both casual walkers and seasoned trekkers.

In the footsteps of ancient heroes, philosophers, and monks, one can't help but feel a profound connection to the land and its history. As you ascend the same trails where, according to the myths, the gods once trod, you may find yourself wondering if that eagle soaring high above is Zeus himself, surveying his divine realm.

The mountainous terrain of the mainland provides an array of exciting challenges. Trails meander through dense forests, cross clear mountain streams, and open up to breathtaking vistas. Among these, the Zagori region in the Pindus mountain range and Mount Olympus, the legendary home of the ancient Greek gods, are unforgettable experiences for any avid trekker.

The Greek islands, too, boast a unique network of paths, offering a chance to explore their often overlooked interior. On islands such as Crete, Naxos, and Andros, treks lead through verdant olive groves, quaint rural villages, and past ancient ruins, revealing a side to the islands far removed from the usual beach scene.

So, pack your hiking boots and prepare to explore Greece in the most adventurous way, one step at a time. Whether it's a gentle stroll or a challenging hike, the rewards are equally gratifying: panoramic views, tranquil nature, archaeological treasures, and the satisfaction of journeying through a landscape steeped in myth and history.

Aegean Water Adventures: Sailing, Diving, Snorkeling

The dazzling blue waters of the Aegean and Ionian seas beckon with the promise of water-based adventures. The Greek seascape, studded with a plethora of islands, hidden coves, and underwater treasures, offers a vibrant playground for maritime pursuits. As you shift your adventure from the rugged mountain paths to the rhythm of the waves, the thrill and tranquility of the Greek seas are sure to captivate you.

Sailing: Voyage of the Argonauts

In a land where seafaring has been ingrained in the culture since the age of myth, embarking on a sailing trip can feel like stepping into a Homeric epic. As the yacht slices through the turquoise waters, the wind filling the sails like the breath of Aeolus, the god of winds, the timelessness of the experience is palpable.

Whether you wish to island-hop through the Cyclades, explore the unspoiled beauty of the Dodecanese, or drop anchor in secluded bays only accessible by sea, sailing offers an unrivaled perspective of Greece's maritime landscapes. Charter a yacht with a skipper or, if you're an experienced sailor, take the helm yourself to chart your course across the Greek seas. The freedom to explore at your own pace, combined with the idyllic scenery, make this one of the most memorable experiences you can have in Greece.

Diving and Snorkeling: Plato's Atlantis Revealed

Beneath the azure surface of the Greek seas lies a world of wonder. Diving and snorkeling in Greece's coastal waters reveal a mesmerizing array of marine life, archaeological treasures, and dramatic underwater landscapes.

The underwater archaeological sites, like the one off the coast of Delos, present a unique opportunity to explore the remnants of ancient civilizations beneath the waves. Here, you'll find sunken city ruins, ancient shipwrecks, and underwater caves adorned with stalactites and stalagmites. The Aegean Sea serves as a vibrant museum, merging history and nature in an exquisite underwater spectacle.

Even without the archaeological sites, the marine biodiversity is captivating. Divers and snorkelers can swim amidst shoals of colorful fish, octopuses, and, if lucky, come face to face with a playful Mediterranean monk seal, one of the world's most endangered marine mammals.

Remember to always adhere to local regulations, dive within your limits, and respect the fragile marine environment. Your underwater adventure could turn out to be the highlight of your Greek journey, an odyssey that carries you into the realm of Poseidon himself.

HELLENIC SPIRIT: FESTIVALS, MUSIC, DANCE

An alluring aspect of Greece that's often nestled deep within the heart of the country is its lively cultural activities. To truly understand the soul of Greece, one must immerse themselves in the rich tapestry of festivals, music, and dance that offer a vibrant expression of its centuries-old traditions and infectious joie de vivre.

Traditional Festivals: A Year-Round Celebration

Greece, where myths blend seamlessly into everyday life, is a country that loves to celebrate. The calendar here brims with traditional festivals (known as "panigiria"), a delightful blend of religious observance, communal feasting, and exuberant merrymaking.

While each festival has its unique charm, they all share certain elements – candlelit processions, the lingering aroma of incense, the infectious sounds of traditional music, local delicacies shared under the starlit sky, and an openness that welcomes every visitor into the heart of the local community.

One of my personal favorites is the August 15th celebration of the Assumption of Virgin Mary, especially on the island of Tinos. Thousands of pilgrims make their way to the sacred Church of Panagia Evangelistria, some even crawling on their knees from the port, in a testament to their faith. The festival atmosphere, combined with the emotional intensity of the pilgrimage, creates a uniquely poignant experience.

Music and Dance: An Ancient Rhythm

Music and dance hold a central place in the heart of the Greek cultural scene, encapsulating the nation's history, spirit, and creative energy. The rhythm of Greece is passionate, heartwarming, and undeniably infectious.

Try attending a live performance of "rebetiko," often called the Greek blues, in a local "rebetadiko." The soul-stirring tunes, born in the urban neighborhoods of Piraeus and Thessaloniki, speak of love, sorrow, and the trials of life, bridging the gap between the past and the present.

And then there's the Greek dance, an expression of joy, camaraderie, and often, the spirit of resistance. It's not uncommon during a Greek festival or even at a taverna, for a casual observer to be swept up in a spontaneous 'panigyri,' a circle of dancers where you link arms and move together to the rhythm of the music. You may stumble over the intricate steps of the "syrtaki" or "tsamiko" at first, but remember - it's all about the shared joy of the moment.

Through the lens of these cultural activities, you'll see Greece in all its timeless glory - a land where the echoes of ancient gods blend with the laughter of today, where traditions are kept alive not just in memories but in the vibrant, living celebration of the present. So, dive in, let your feet follow the rhythm, and your heart the melody. Who knows? You may find a piece of your own spirit dancing under the Grecian sky.

ADVENTURE SPORTS: EMBRACING THE THRILL OF GREECE

For the adrenaline junkies and thrill-seekers among you, Greece is not just a haven of culture and history, but also a playground filled with action and adventure. The diverse terrain of Greece, from its rugged mountains to its azure seas, offers endless possibilities for exhilarating outdoor pursuits. Let me take you on a journey through some of my favorite adventure sports in Greece, intertwining personal experiences with helpful hints and tips.

Mountain Biking: On the Trails of Mount Olympus

Picture this: you, your mountain bike, and the trails of Mount Olympus, the legendary home of the Greek gods. Mountain biking in Greece is an experience like no other. As you navigate through the lush forests and challenging trails of Mount Olympus, you're not only getting a healthy dose of adrenaline but also an up-close encounter with Greek mythology.

A particularly memorable experience for me was conquering the challenging Enipeas Gorge trail. The rough terrain made for a testing journey, but the breathtaking views of the mythical mountain were worth every drop of sweat. There are multiple bike rental and tour agencies catering to all skill levels, but do ensure you're in good physical condition and equipped with protective gear.

Rock Climbing: Scaling the Heights of Meteora

Meteora, with its towering rock formations and historical monasteries, provides a unique rock climbing experience. Whether you're an experienced climber or a novice, the rock pillars of Meteora offer routes for all skill levels.

My first climb here, despite being an avid climber, was humbling. The awe-inspiring view of the monasteries perched precariously atop the rocks served as a beautiful distraction. Local climbing schools offer lessons and equipment rental, making this an accessible adventure sport for all.

Windsurfing and Kitesurfing: Riding the Aegean Winds

For water sports enthusiasts, the Aegean Islands are the place to be, with their reliable summer winds providing perfect conditions for windsurfing and kitesurfing. The island of Rhodes, particularly Prasonisi Bay, is a hot spot for these sports.

I remember the first time I tried windsurfing in Prasonisi – the thrill of harnessing the wind's power and gliding over the waves was exhilarating. For beginners, local schools offer lessons that ensure you understand the safety protocols while helping you master the basics.

Paragliding: Soaring Over the Ionian Islands

There's nothing quite like the freedom of paragliding over the stunning Ionian Islands. I took my first flight from the hills of Lefkada, soaring over turquoise waters and picturesque landscapes, a memory I hold dear. Several companies offer tandem paragliding experiences, allowing you to enjoy the vistas safely under the guidance of an experienced professional.

From land to sea and even air, Greece's adventure sports opportunities are diverse and thrilling. My advice? Don't hesitate to step out of your comfort zone – you never know what unforgettable experience awaits in this land of gods and heroes. After all, what's life without a little adventure?

AERIAL VIEW OF PORTO TIMONI, AFIONAS

Chapter 14: Packing Tips for Greece: A Savvy Traveler's Guide

*P*acking for a journey abroad, especially to a destination as multifaceted as Greece, can sometimes feel like a Herculean task. Each region, each season, and each type of activity calls for different essentials, and it can be a tricky balance to pack both pragmatically and efficiently. As a seasoned traveler, I've had my fair share of packing mishaps and triumphs, learning along the way the art of preparing just the right suitcase for a Greek escapade. This chapter is dedicated to sharing my tried-and-true packing tips, tailor-made for Greece, to help you focus less on the stress of packing and more on the excitement of your upcoming journey.

What to Pack for Different Seasons: Understanding Greece's Climate

Spring (March-May):

Springtime in Greece is enchanting, with landscapes awash in blooming flowers and a pleasant warmth in the air. The daytime temperatures start to rise, averaging between 15-25°C, but the evenings can still be relatively cool, especially in the northern regions and the islands.

For this season, I recommend packing a mix of light clothing for the warmer days, such as t-shirts, long-sleeve shirts, jeans, and comfortable walking shoes. A light jacket or sweater will also come in handy for cooler nights. If you plan on visiting religious sites, remember to bring attire that covers your shoulders and knees. An umbrella is worth including for the occasional spring showers.

Summer (June-August):

Greek summers are renowned for their brilliant sunshine and high temperatures, often reaching upwards of 30°C, particularly on the islands and in southern mainland Greece. It's the perfect season for beach hopping and island exploration, but the heat can be intense.

Packing for summer in Greece is all about sun protection and comfort. Include plenty of lightweight, breathable clothing in your suitcase—linen shirts, cotton dresses, and shorts are great choices. Don't forget your swimwear, a wide-brimmed hat, sunglasses, and a good SPF sunscreen. A pair of comfortable sandals is also a must for those strolls along the cobblestone streets of charming island towns.

Autumn (September-November):

Autumn sees a gradual cooling from the intense heat of summer, with temperatures ranging between 15-25°C. The sea remains warm enough for swimming well into

September, and the changing colors of the landscapes make for scenic hiking and sightseeing.

In this season, pack similar to springtime but consider including a slightly warmer jacket or coat, particularly for November when temperatures can drop. Layers are key as the temperature can fluctuate throughout the day. Rain can also be more frequent during the fall, so a lightweight, packable rain jacket could be a valuable addition.

Winter (December-February):

Winter in Greece is mild compared to many northern European countries. Coastal areas experience temperatures between 10-15°C, while mountainous areas and northern Greece can see colder temperatures, even snowfall.

Winter packing should include warm clothing—thermal layers, sweaters, a warm coat, and a good pair of shoes for potentially wet conditions. If you're heading to the mountains, you'll want warmer gear, possibly including a hat, gloves, and a scarf. Even in winter, the Greek sun can be strong, so don't leave your sunglasses at home.

In all seasons, remember to pack any necessary medications, travel documents, and a good guidebook—perhaps this one you're reading right now! Also, a universal adapter will be needed for your electronics as Greece uses Type C and Type F plugs. Lastly, keep in mind that less is more—Greece is known for its casual, laid-back style, so focus on comfort and functionality over extravagance. Happy packing!

ESSENTIAL ITEMS TO INCLUDE: KEY NECESSITIES FOR A SMOOTH GREEK ADVENTURE

While packing for any trip requires considering the usual suspects - clothing, toiletries, and important documents - there are some items that are particularly handy when it comes to traversing the Greek landscapes. These are the essentials I've found to be invaluable in my countless journeys to this spectacular country:

Comfortable Footwear: I remember a trip to Athens when a companion of mine underestimated the amount of walking we'd do. Let's just say the brand-new, stylish, yet decidedly uncomfortable shoes he packed did him no favors. Greece is full of cobblestone streets, stairs, and hills. Whether you're exploring the historical sites of Athens or the steep, winding lanes of Santorini, a pair of sturdy, comfortable shoes will be your best friend.

Sun Protection: The Greek sun is no joke, especially during the summer months. A broad-brimmed hat, sunglasses, and a quality sunscreen with high SPF are non-negotiables. I still recall the summer day I spent at Elafonisi beach, mesmerized by the turquoise waters and without realizing, had missed reapplying my sunscreen. My lobster-red skin was a painful reminder for the rest of the trip!

Swimwear: Whether it's taking a dip in the crystal-clear waters of Mykonos or partaking in a soothing swim in the hot springs of Santorini, you're going to want to pack your favorite swimwear—and perhaps an extra pair or two. An easy-to-carry beach towel is also a good idea.

Power Adapter: Greece uses Type C and Type F outlets, different from many other countries. Pack a universal adapter to ensure you can keep your devices charged. Trust me, the last thing you want is to run out of battery power while capturing that perfect sunset shot in Oia!

Light Layers: As I've mentioned earlier, the weather can fluctuate quite a bit in Greece, particularly between day and night. Packing lightweight layers will allow you to adapt to changing temperatures.

Travel Insurance Documents: A lesson I learned the hard way was the importance of having copies of your travel insurance documents on hand. When I had a minor mishap with a motorbike in Crete, having those documents easily accessible made dealing with the hospital a lot smoother.

Portable Power Bank: On an exciting day exploring Delphi, my phone died just when I was about to take a picture with the Temple of Apollo in the backdrop. Now, I never travel without a portable power bank. With long days of exploration and picture-taking, this device is a lifesaver.

Quick-dry Towel and Water Shoes: These are particularly handy if you plan on engaging in water sports or island-hopping. Many of the beaches in Greece are pebbly, and water shoes can make your beach visits more comfortable.

Remember, your journey through Greece should be one of joy and discovery, not discomfort or inconvenience. By ensuring you have these essentials in your suitcase, you'll be setting yourself up for a truly memorable Greek adventure.

TRAVELING RESPONSIBLY IN GREECE: A JOURNEY TOWARDS SUSTAINABLE TOURISM

One of my most cherished memories in Greece was in a small, family-run taverna on the island of Paros. As I relished a meal of freshly caught octopus and locally-grown olives, I struck up a conversation with the owner. He spoke passionately about the importance of preserving the traditions and environment that make Greece so unique. That night, I left the taverna with more than a full stomach—I left with a renewed appreciation for the role of responsible tourism in protecting these precious elements.

As travelers, we have the power to make a positive impact on the destinations we visit. In Greece, this means embracing sustainable practices that conserve its natural beauty, respect its cultural heritage, and support its local communities. Here are some key ways we can travel responsibly in this extraordinary country:

Support Local Businesses: Opt for family-run tavernas over large chain restaurants, shop for crafts in local boutiques instead of mass-market stores, and choose accommodations owned by locals. Not only will this enrich your travel experience, but it will also provide essential support to the local economy.

Respect Cultural Norms: Greeks are known for their hospitality and warmth, but it's important to respect local customs and traditions. Dress modestly when visiting monasteries and churches, and remember to ask for permission before photographing people. One time, I made the mistake of attempting to enter the Monastery of the Holy Trinity in Meteora in shorts and had to sheepishly return to my car to change. A quick study of local norms can save both embarrassment and potential offense.

Minimize Environmental Impact: Carry a reusable water bottle to avoid single-use plastic, and remember to dispose of your waste properly. The Greek islands are renowned for their pristine landscapes—let's do our part to keep them that way. During a visit to Naxos, I was part of a beach clean-up organized by a local environmental group. It was a stark reminder of the importance of minimizing our impact and leaving no trace.

Preserve Historical Sites: The archaeological treasures of Greece are a legacy from the past that we're privileged to witness. Don't climb on ancient structures, and never remove stones or artifacts from these sites. When I visited the ancient city of Delphi, I was awed by the grandeur of the Temple of Apollo. It's critical that we preserve these historical marvels for future generations.

Use Resources Wisely: Conserve water and energy as much as possible. This is particularly important during the summer months when resources can be scarce. On my journey through Crete, I was mindful to take quick showers and turn off the air conditioning when leaving the room.

Travel Off the Beaten Path: One of my most rewarding Greek experiences was exploring the lesser-known town of Nafpaktos in western Greece. By venturing beyond the typical tourist trails, we can distribute tourism's impacts more evenly and discover the hidden gems of the country.

Traveling responsibly in Greece, or anywhere else for that matter, is not merely an obligation—it's a commitment to preserving the places we love so they can continue to inspire travelers for generations to come. Let's carry this commitment in our hearts as we journey through the wondrous landscapes of Greece.

CHAPTER 15 - EXPLORING THE LESSER - KNOWN ISLANDS: THE HIDDEN GEMS OF GREECE

Greece, the allure of this ancient land is impossible to contain within mere chapters. The country's charm extends far beyond the familiar tales of Athens, Santorini, or Mykonos. The real magic of Greece is also nestled in its lesser-known islands, each a hidden gem waiting to reveal its secrets to the intrepid traveler. It is here, away from the bustling tourist paths, that you might truly connect with the soul of Greece.

Just as a seasoned sailor navigates the sea using the stars, let me guide you through the scattered islands of Greece, where you can chart your own course.

As we continue this voyage to the lesser-known islands of Greece, it's impossible not to feel the immense breadth and depth of the country's charm that is so deeply intertwined with its landscape and history.

FOLEGANDROS: THE ISLAND OF PEACE

When you first set foot on the tranquil island of Folegandros, you are immediately greeted with a sense of tranquillity that the modern world often lacks. A place where time appears to stand still, it remains remarkably untouched by the bustle of mass tourism, offering a peaceful retreat for those seeking solitude.

On one of my numerous visits to this enchanting island, I remember climbing up to the cliff-top church of Panagia, perched high above the capital town of Chora. The serenity of that moment, paired with the panoramic view of the vast Aegean Sea stretching into infinity, was something out of a dream. The church, radiant in the soft light of the setting sun, seemed to be guarding the island's traditional way of life, far removed from the worries of the outside world.

As you explore this serene haven, you will come across a variety of picturesque scenes: narrow cobblestone streets lined with whitewashed houses draped in bougainvillea, the old castle offering magnificent views of the island, and small, secluded beaches where the only sounds are of gentle waves caressing the shore.

One such beach is Agali, a beautiful cove with crystal clear turquoise waters, perfect for a refreshing swim. Just around the corner is the charming taverna where Maria, a local woman with an infectious smile, serves her homemade moussaka. The enticing aroma of her cooking, combined with the natural beauty of the setting, is a feast for all the senses.

Folegandros also takes pride in its traditional feasts or "paniyiria", celebrations that revolve around the island's churches. During these feasts, locals and visitors gather to enjoy local music, dancing, and food under the starlit sky. As the island's folk music echoes through the night, you are reminded of the strong sense of community that binds this little island together.

In Folegandros, you don't just find a beautiful Greek island; you discover a sanctuary, a place where simplicity and tranquillity reign. Each visit leaves you with a renewed sense of peace and an intimate understanding of the island's unique charm. Its tranquillity is not just a state but a lifestyle, a precious gift for the weary soul, making every moment spent on this island a treasured memory.

ITHACA: THE LAND OF ODYSSEUS

If you are a fan of epic tales, a visit to Ithaca will resonate deeply. Known as the home of Odysseus, the hero of Homer's Odyssey, Ithaca is steeped in myth and legend. The island is a paradise for explorers, with its hidden coves, verdant hills, and archaeological sites whispering tales of yore. While the island may lack the grandeur of larger destinations, it more than makes up for it with its raw, untouched beauty and deep cultural roots.

ALONISSOS: A NATURAL RETREAT

Nestled in the heart of the National Marine Park of the Northern Sporades, the greenest island in the Aegean, Alonissos, is a treasure trove of natural beauty. Its rich flora and fauna, including the Mediterranean monk seal, make it a haven for nature lovers. My most cherished memory of Alonissos is a kayak trip along its stunning coastline, dotted with secret caves and deserted beaches, an experience I recommend with heartfelt enthusiasm.

As you venture into these lesser-known islands of Greece, remember that each island, like each traveler, has its own story to tell. Listen to their tales, engage with the locals, savour their gastronomy, immerse yourself in their culture, and leave each place having grown from the experience.

AMORGOS: THE ISLAND OF DEEP BLUE

A significant distance from Athens, this island remains a well-kept secret, evading the grasp of mainstream tourism. Here you'll find monasteries precariously clinging to cliffs, ancient footpaths leading you through wildflower-strewn landscapes, and the striking Big Blue – yes, that endless azure sea which was famously depicted in Luc Besson's film "The Big Blue". It is impossible to forget your first time witnessing the sunlight playing on the surface of the sea, transforming it into an artist's palette of blues. A scuba diving trip here, off the shores of the enchanting beach of Mouros, remains one of my most cherished underwater experiences.

KYTHIRA: THE CELESTIAL ISLAND

Tucked away at the southern tip of the Peloponnese, Kythira is a place of wild beauty and divine legends. Known as the celestial island of the goddess Aphrodite, it lures visitors with its cascading waterfalls, ancient ruins, and charming villages. Each turn on this island offers a new discovery: from the vibrant square of Chora filled with local artists displaying their works, to the mystical ambiance of the Cave of Agia Sofia, with its beautiful frescoes.

There is a powerful sense of reverence that resonates through the island – perhaps a touch of the divine Aphrodite herself.

SYROS: THE ISLAND OF HIDDEN GRANDEUR

Despite being the capital of the Cyclades, Syros remains less frequented by tourists, a fact which only adds to its allure. Here, the past and present converge seamlessly. The island's capital, Ermoupoli, is an architectural marvel with its neoclassical mansions and grand squares. While exploring the streets of this beautiful city, I came upon a spontaneous performance by a local music school – the melodies of the Greek bouzouki filling the air is a memory that still warms my heart.

KOS: THE HEALING ISLAND

The island of Kos, famously known as the birthplace of Hippocrates, the father of medicine, is yet another off-the-beaten-path gem to consider for your Greek odyssey. Rich in history, vibrant in culture, and blessed with natural beauty, Kos offers a taste of the quintessential Greek island experience.

As you step onto the island, a sense of its historical grandeur unfolds. Here, in the ancient town of Kos, you'll find the Tree of Hippocrates, a magnificent plane tree under which Hippocrates allegedly taught his students. Although the current tree is only about 500 years old, the symbolism and the ancient ruins surrounding it breathe life into the legend. My first visit to Kos was filled with such discoveries. As I cycled along the flat cycling paths that crisscross the island, I came upon the Asklepieion, an ancient healing temple dedicated to Asclepius, the god of medicine. Exploring the terraced ruins with the sweeping views of the Turkish coast across the Aegean Sea was truly awe-inspiring.

But Kos isn't just about history and healing; it's also about enjoying the sea, sun, and sand. Kos offers a wide range of beach experiences, from the busy Lambi beach with a multitude of cafes and restaurants to the quieter, family-friendly Tigaki beach.

For those seeking an authentic adventure, the secluded Agios Theologos beach, with its pebbles, pristine waters, and dramatic waves, is a must-visit.

During my stay in Kos, I found myself drawn to its vibrant culinary scene. Local tavernas serve delicious traditional dishes, while modern restaurants offer innovative takes on Greek cuisine. One such memorable meal was at a family-owned taverna in the village of Zia, where I enjoyed succulent 'lamb Kleftiko' under the shade of grapevines, overlooking a breathtaking sunset.

Cultural life in Kos is colorful and dynamic, epitomized by the lively festivals held throughout the summer. These 'panigiria' are brimming with traditional music, dance, and a shared feast of local delicacies, providing a snapshot of the island's community spirit.

Kos is an island where ancient history and modern life beautifully coexist, where every road can lead to a new adventure. Whether you're seeking an active holiday, a journey through history, or simply a tranquil getaway, Kos promises a memorable and enriching experience. As I boarded the ferry back to mainland Greece, I carried with me the memories of an island that had touched my soul, promising myself to return to its welcoming shores.

Remember, as an explorer of these lesser-known islands, you are not just a visitor but an active participant in their narratives. Soak in the peace of Folegandros, trace the path of Odysseus in Ithaca, become one with nature in Alonissos, lose yourself in the deep blue of Amorgos, feel the divine touch in Kythira, and listen to the music of life in Syros.

These experiences, these islands, form the invisible thread that connects the heart of Greece with those willing to venture off the beaten path. By exploring these hidden gems, you are embarking on an intimate journey that whispers the stories of ancient gods, adventurous heroes, and the unyielding spirit of the Greek people.

The beauty of Greece is as vast as the Aegean itself, and these lesser-known islands are but a glimpse into its rich tapestry. With each footstep on their cobbled streets and each gaze upon their endless horizons, you'll be writing your own epic in the land where stories were born.

In the end, your heart will be full of not just memories, but stories - stories of places discovered, of friendships forged, of cultures celebrated, and of a Greece that resides not only in maps but also in the heartbeats of its islands.

ANCIENT RUINS ON KOS

CHAPTER 16 - THE WINES OF GREECE

In a country famous for its food, Greece's unique and flavorful wines should not be overlooked. Steeped in history and enhanced by the diverse terroirs, Greek wines carry the whispers of mythology, the echoes of the ancient world, and the pulse of modern viticulture. Whether you're an oenophile or a casual wine enthusiast, this chapter aims to take you on a journey through the vineyards of Greece. We'll explore the history of winemaking, the country's key wine regions, and of course, the unique varietals that the Greek soil gifts us. We'll also delve into wine tasting and vineyard tours that enrich your travel experience, and I'll share some tips on pairing Greek wines with the local cuisine to elevate your gastronomic adventure.

INTRODUCTION TO GREEK WINE HISTORY

Nowhere else is the history of wine so intertwined with the culture and mythology of a place. In Greece, **wine has been cultivated for over 4000 years**, making it one of the oldest wine-producing regions in the world. Dionysus, the Greek god of the grape harvest, wine, and winemaking, played a significant role in ancient Greek culture. His celebrations were a pivotal part of the society, and this deep cultural link continues to influence Greek winemaking traditions today. Greek wine was central to ancient society, used in religious ceremonies, and shared at gatherings. Amphoras (clay vessels) filled with wine were traded across the ancient world, spreading Greek viticulture. Through the ups and downs of history - the Roman period, the Byzantine era, Ottoman rule, and into modern times - the vine has persisted as a symbol of Greek resilience and love for the land.

The modern era of Greek wine began in the 1960s, with the emergence of new wineries focusing on native varietals and terroir. This led to a renaissance in Greek wine, which continues today, with a new generation of winemakers dedicated to creating wines that truly express the character of Greece's diverse regions. As you sip a glass of Greek wine, remember: you're not just enjoying a drink, but partaking in a story that's thousands of years old, a true liquid history. So, let's raise a glass, or as the Greeks say, "Yamas!" (Cheers), to the enduring tradition of Greek winemaking!

Varietals and Wine Regions

Understanding the Greek wine scene starts with familiarizing oneself with its varietals and key wine regions. Here's a closer look at the diverse array of Greek wines and where they originate from:

Assyrtiko (Santorini and other islands)

One of the country's most famous white varietals, Assyrtiko, originates from the volcanic soils of Santorini. It produces dry, full-bodied whites with a distinctive mineral character and a unique hint of salinity - a testament to the island's sea-lashed terroirs.

Moschofilero (Peloponnese)

This pink-skinned grape from the mountainous region of Peloponnese is known for its delightful floral and spicy white wines. The cooler temperatures in the Mantinia plateau impart an invigorating acidity to Moschofilero wines.

Agiorgitiko (Nemea, Peloponnese)

Often referred to as "Saint George," Agiorgitiko is the most widely planted red grape in Greece. It's native to Nemea in the Peloponnese and produces wines that range from fresh, fruity rosés to complex, age-worthy reds.

Xinomavro (Naoussa, Northern Greece)

Xinomavro is the king of reds in the cooler northern regions of Greece. Its name means "acid black," reflecting the wine's high acidity and deep color. Xinomavro wines are known for their rich, complex flavors, often compared to Italy's Nebbiolo.

These are just a few examples of the fascinating variety in Greek wine. Each region has its unique varietals, creating an intriguing patchwork of flavors across the Greek landscape. So, don't stop at tasting just one or two – every bottle offers a new discovery, a different story of the Greek land and its ancient viticulture.

The true magic of Greek wine comes alive when you step into its wineries and vineyards. There's something incredibly special about sipping a glass of wine in the very place where the grapes grow, getting a glimpse into the winemaking process, and understanding the story behind each bottle. If you are a wine enthusiast, here are some key vineyard tours and tasting experiences you must consider:

Santorini's Volcanic Vineyards

On this sun-kissed island, grapes are grown in a unique basket-shaped pattern, close to the ground to protect them from the wind. Visiting vineyards in Santorini and tasting its signature Assyrtiko wine is a sensory journey you won't forget.

Nemea's Renowned Wineries

Nemea is one of the most important wine-producing regions in Greece. Here, you can explore a variety of wineries that produce the exceptional Agiorgitiko wine. A tour around Nemea offers an enriching journey through the lush vineyards and the opportunity to meet local winemakers who are passionately carrying forward Greece's winemaking heritage.

Naoussa's Wine Trail

If you appreciate red wines with a robust character, then touring the vineyards in Naoussa, Northern Greece, should be on your agenda. Home to the Xinomavro varietal, you can embark on a wine trail that takes you through rustic wineries and sprawling vineyards, offering a first-hand taste of this region's dynamic wine culture.

Wine Tasting in the Peloponnese

With a wine history dating back four thousand years, the Peloponnese peninsula is a treat for wine lovers. Don't miss the chance to taste the vibrant Moschofilero wines in the high-altitude vineyards of Mantinia.

Taking part in wine tasting and vineyard tours is more than just about sampling different wines. It's about immersing yourself in Greek culture, discovering the unique terroirs, understanding the rich history, and appreciating the dedication and passion of the winemakers. It's an unforgettable experience that will add another dimension to your Greek odyssey.

Food and wine share an intimate relationship in Greece. The local cuisine, with its sun-kissed flavors, and the diversity of Greek wines create a synergy that takes the gastronomic experience to a whole new level. Whether you're indulging in a beachside taverna or a chic city eatery, knowing how to pair Greek wines with traditional dishes will elevate your dining experiences:

Assyrtiko and Fresh Seafood

Starting with the crisp white wines of Greece, Assyrtiko from Santorini is a delightful pairing with seafood. Its high acidity and mineral notes are a great counterbalance to the freshness of calamari, oysters, or a simple grilled fish.

Agiorgitiko and Lamb

For the red wine lovers, Agiorgitiko (St. George's grape), is an absolute treat when paired with a traditional Greek lamb dish. The wine's velvety tannins and aromatic complexity complement the rich flavors of lamb perfectly, whether it's in a stew or roasted.

Moschofilero and Greek Salads

The vibrant Moschofilero white wines from the Peloponnese, with their floral and citrusy notes, are ideal for light dishes like Greek salads. The crisp acidity cuts through the richness of feta cheese, making each bite even more refreshing.

Xinomavro and Moussaka

Xinomavro, a versatile red wine with a robust character, pairs remarkably well with hearty dishes like moussaka. The wine's tannic structure and acidity are just the right match for the dish's creamy béchamel sauce and spiced meat filling.

Vinsanto and Baklava

No meal in Greece is complete without a sweet ending. The dessert wine Vinsanto from Santorini, with its luscious notes of dried fruits, honey, and spices, is a heavenly match with baklava or other honey-drizzled Greek pastries.

*Remember, **wine pairing** is not about strict rules but about harmonizing flavors and enhancing your overall dining experience. When in doubt, ask the locals or your hosts for their recommendations - their insightful tips might introduce you to pairings that you've never thought of before. Enjoy the journey of flavors and aromas, as each pairing tells a unique story of Greece's culinary and winemaking tradition.*

CHAPTER 17 - GREEK FESTIVALS AND CELEBRATIONS

*T*he Greek calendar is dotted with numerous festivals and celebrations, deeply ingrained in the country's rich history and vibrant culture. These events range from religious holidays to regional festivals, each offering a unique spectacle of traditions, rituals, music, and food. Here's a closer look at some of the most significant celebrations that you might want to align your travels with:

Easter: Greece's Biggest Holiday

Orthodox Easter is the most important celebration in Greece, even surpassing Christmas in terms of grandeur and spiritual significance. The Holy Week leading up to Easter Sunday is a time of devout prayer, fasting, and solemn processions. However, the culmination of Lent on Easter Sunday sees the whole country erupting into joyous celebrations. Lamb is roasted on a spit, red-dyed eggs are cracked in a symbol of Christ's resurrection, and the

Apokries: Greek Carnival

Apokries, the Greek Carnival, is another vibrant and much-anticipated event in the Greek calendar. This three-week period leading up to Lent is a time of masquerade and revelry, where cities and islands alike dress up in a colourful blend of Venetian and local folkloric traditions. The city of Patras hosts the biggest carnival, but Rethymno in Crete and the island of Skyros have their unique twists. Expect magnificent parades, masquerade balls, and a lot of dancing, with a lively, all-encompassing atmosphere that invites you to let loose and join in. Even if you're not typically one for large gatherings, the communal joy and centuries-old customs that come to life during Apokries are a truly captivating sight.

The August Moon Festival

The August Moon Festival is a cultural staple and one of the most beautiful events of the Greek summer. Coinciding with the full moon in August, the festival takes advantage of the beautiful Mediterranean nights, when the moon illuminates the Aegean Sea, casting a magical glow. Many archaeological sites, such as the Acropolis in Athens, the ancient site of Philippi in Kavala, and the Palace of the Grand Master in Rhodes, stay open late and often host concerts, theatrical performances, and other events. It's a remarkable experience, offering a unique perspective on these iconic sites under the enchanting moonlit sky.

Ochi Day: Celebrating Greek Independence

Ochi Day, observed on October 28th, commemorates Greece's brave refusal of Mussolini's ultimatum in 1940, marking the nation's entry into World War II on the Allied side. This national holiday is a day of pride and resilience, filled with parades and celebrations throughout the country. Military parades are the highlight in bigger cities, whereas schoolchildren's parades take place in smaller towns. It's an opportunity for Greeks to honour their history and pay tribute to their heroes. For travellers, Ochi Day offers an insight into the country's national spirit and its people's passionate dedication to their heritage.

Stay tuned for our last celebration feature, a staple of the Greek community life, known as Panigyria in our next section.

Panigyria: The Soul of Greek Village Festivals

Amidst the tapestry of Greek festivities, Panigyria holds a special place. Often associated with rural and island communities, Panigyria are traditional, communal festivals celebrated in honor of a local saint, the Virgin Mary, or Christ. These festivals, however, are not just religious affairs. They encapsulate the spirit of togetherness, as entire villages or island communities come together in a vibrant blend of devotion, music, dance, and gastronomy. The day typically begins with a church service, paying respects to the patron saint. As the sun sets, the atmosphere undergoes a transformative shift. Makeshift tavernas spring up, serving local delicacies and free-flowing wine. Musicians strike up tunes with traditional instruments like the bouzouki, lira, and tambourine, setting feet tapping and hearts racing. As the music crescendos, impromptu dance circles form, with people holding hands, dancing in unison, and celebrating life in its purest form.

Each Panigyri offers a unique experience, often influenced by the region's specific customs and traditions. For travelers, attending one is akin to taking a deep dive into the heart of Greek culture. It's a glimpse into an age-old tradition where joy, community spirit, and faith converge. If you ever find yourself in Greece during a Panigyri, don't hesitate to join in. You'll be welcomed with open arms into a celebration that continues until the first light of dawn.

Chapter 18 - A Deeper Look at Greek Traditions

*T*raditions, they say, are the threads that weave together the rich tapestry of a culture. In Greece, this tapestry is vibrant, intricate, and steeped in history. Greek traditions are a blend of the country's ancient past and its modern spirit, a beautiful dance between the old and the new that is as enchanting as the land itself. In this chapter, we aim to take you on a journey through some of the most fascinating aspects of Greek culture that continue to shape the nation's way of life. We will explore the importance of the Greek Siesta, the celebratory nature of Greek Name Days, the mystery surrounding the evil eye superstition, the ethos of Filotimo, and the soul-stirring sounds of Greek music. Whether you're planning a trip or just looking to deepen your understanding of this incredible country, delving into these traditions will provide a meaningful context to your Greek experience. So, come along as we step into the heart of Greece and uncover the cultural treasures that make this land so extraordinarily captivating.

The Greek Siesta

Ah, the Greek siesta, a wonderful tradition that truly epitomizes the country's dedication to the art of relaxation. The siesta is a midday break, typically lasting from 2 pm to 5 pm, where businesses shutter their doors, and the streets become unusually quiet. The purpose of this break isn't simply a nap - though that is certainly a part of it for some - but a time to escape the afternoon heat, enjoy a leisurely lunch, and spend quality time with family. This custom of a daily pause in activity has roots in antiquity, with references dating back to Homer's times, and it aligns perfectly with the Mediterranean climate where the midday sun can be sweltering. While the tradition has faded in the major cities due to modern work schedules, it still thrives in smaller towns and islands. So, when in Greece, don't be surprised if you find the stores closed in the afternoon. Just embrace the rhythm of the day and enjoy your own little siesta.

Greek Name Days

While birthdays are celebrated worldwide, Greeks place a higher importance on Name Days. A name day, or "Onomastiki Eorti," is the day dedicated to the saint that an individual is named after. For instance, if you're named George, your name day would be April 23rd, the Feast of St. George. These celebrations often involve open house parties where friends and relatives drop by uninvited for food, wine, and merrymaking. It's a unique aspect of Greek culture and a testament to the strong ties between their religious beliefs and social life.

The Evil Eye: A Greek Superstition

In Greek culture, the "evil eye," or "mati," is a look given to inflict harm, suffering, or some form of bad luck on those that it is cast upon. This belief is deeply rooted in Greek society and dates back to ancient times. To ward off the evil eye, Greeks often wear a charm known as the "matiasma," a blue glass bead with an eye design, believed to offer protection against this malevolent gaze. Even if you're not superstitious, it's hard not to get drawn into the compelling mythology surrounding this age-old Greek superstition.

Filotimo: The Greek Love of Honor

Filotimo is a Greek concept that can't be directly translated into English, but it's a vital part of Greek social interaction. It involves a mix of values like honor, dignity, sacrifice, and respect for others. It's about doing what's right without expecting anything in return. Filotimo is at the heart of how Greeks interact with their families, neighbors, and even strangers, reflecting a strong sense of community spirit and social responsibility. It's a testament to the character of the Greek people and their dedication to social harmony and mutual respect.

Greek Music: From Bouzouki to Rembetika

Music is an integral part of Greek culture, expressing the country's historical struggles, joys, and unique spirit. Whether it's the stringed melodies of the bouzouki, the soulful tunes of Rembetika (often referred to as the Greek blues), or the lively rhythms of traditional folk dances, Greek music is a testament to the country's rich cultural heritage. Attending a live music event or even a spontaneous street performance can be a highlight of your Greek journey, offering a chance to connect with the country's culture on a deeply emotional level.

These elements of Greek tradition offer us a glimpse into the heart of Greek society. They shape the rhythm of daily life, infusing it with a sense of community, spirituality, and joy. When you visit Greece, you're not merely stepping into a country; you're stepping into a living, breathing narrative that's been unfolding for millennia. And it's these traditions, these threads of the societal fabric, that make Greece not just a destination, but a truly unique experience.

CHAPTER 19 - UNVEILING GREEK MUSIC AND DANCE

*E*mbarking on a journey through the rich tapestry of Greek music and dance is akin to stepping back in time. These vibrant art forms, deeply ingrained in the country's cultural fabric, are vital expressions of Greek identity, emotion, and communal connection. They reflect Greece's unyielding zest for life and profound appreciation for beauty in all its forms.

The melodic lull of a bouzouki under the moonlit sky, the passionate strumming of a lyre in a bustling marketplace, or the rhythmic clap of hands accompanying a traditional syrtaki dance in a village square - these are the sounds and movements that echo the soul of Greece. In this chapter, we will delve deeper into this entrancing world, tracing the historical evolution of Greek music and dance, spotlighting some of Greece's most influential artists, and guiding you through the country's most compelling music and dance festivals.

Moreover, we'll offer tips on how you can immerse yourself in these jubilant expressions of Hellenic spirit, even giving you the opportunity to learn and participate in these art forms yourself. Let the music guide us, as we journey through the captivating universe of Greek music and dance.

THE HISTORY AND EVOLUTION OF GREEK MUSIC

Our exploration begins in the realm of ancient Greece, where music was an integral part of everyday life. It played a pivotal role in social, religious, and political spheres - from hymns sung in honor of the gods, to melodies accompanying epic poetry, to the music that filled the air at weddings, funerals, and festivals.

As centuries passed, Greek music evolved, imbibing influences from various conquering forces and regions. The Byzantine period introduced a unique form of ecclesiastical music, while the Ottoman rule brought an infusion of Eastern music aesthetics, shaping two forms of music that have become the pillars of Greek music: "Dimotiká" (folk music) and "Éntekhno" (art music).

"Dimotiká", the traditional folk music of rural Greece, is as diverse as the many regions of Greece itself. Ranging from simple love songs to complex dance cycles, this music genre is often accompanied by traditional instruments like the "bouzouki", a type of Greek mandolin, and the "baglamas", a smaller version of the bouzouki.

"Éntekhno" songs, on the other hand, represent a synthesis of Greek folk melodies, Byzantine liturgical music, and Western classical music. These are often complex orchestral pieces that incorporate poetic lyrics and address themes such as love, sorrow, and social issues.

In the 20th century, the urban working classes of Greece gave birth to a unique genre known as "Rebetiko". Often termed the 'Greek Blues,' Rebetiko originated in the refugee camps and shantytowns of Piraeus, the port of Athens. The lyrics of Rebetiko songs often deal with themes of hardship, love, loss, and the harsh realities of life in the urban underworld.

Exploring the World of Greek Dance

Greek dance, much like its music, is a rich and diverse form of cultural expression. It is a tapestry woven with threads of history, tradition, and communal bonding. Greek dance is not just an art; it is a living, breathing part of Greek societal and community life, a testament to the Greek spirit of unity and celebration.

From the energetic steps of the Sirtaki to the swift movements of the Kalamatianos, Greek dances narrate tales of history, passion, joy, and the collective spirit of its people. Greece is home to more than 4,000 traditional dances, each rooted in local customs, folklore, and regional history.

Dances like the Kalamatianos, Tsifteteli, and Zebekiko, each with their unique rhythms and movements, tell the stories of different parts of Greece. Each dance is a vibrant expression of Greek life, from the sensual rhythm of Tsifteteli to the expressive improvisation of Zebekiko. And the Sirtaki, popularized worldwide by the 1964 film "Zorba the Greek", is a perfect introduction to the world of Greek dance for any visitor.

Immerse Yourself in Greek Music and Dance

Learning and participating in Greek dances is a fantastic way to immerse oneself in Greek culture. Numerous festivals, especially during summer, offer dance performances, and some even provide workshops for visitors to learn and participate.

As we delve deeper into the history, evolution, and cultural significance of Greek music and dance, we aim to help you navigate through the country's vibrant musical landscape. As you explore Greece, let the music play, the dancers dance, and your heart resonate with the rhythm of Greek life. Allow yourself to become immersed in the profound and jubilant expressions of Hellenic spirit that are so integral to the country's cultural identity.

Whether you are swaying to the melancholic strains of a bouzouki under a moonlit sky or joining in the lively steps of a traditional syrtaki dance in a village square, you are sure to carry these enchanting melodies and rhythms with you, long after your Greek holiday concludes.

CHAPTER 20 - UNDERSTANDING GREEK PHILOSOPHY

*G*reek philosophy is not simply a collection of abstract theories and metaphysical postulates. It is the cornerstone of Greek civilization, a testament to the intellectual rigor and the spirit of inquiry that have characterized this nation since antiquity. This philosophical tradition, with its profound insights and groundbreaking ideas, has shaped Western thought in ways that can still be felt today.

THE FOUNDATIONS OF GREEK PHILOSOPHY

The birth of philosophy in Greece was driven by a desire to understand the world and our place in it. Greek philosophers sought natural explanations for phenomena that had previously been attributed to the whims of the gods. This fundamental shift in perspective, which occurred around the 6th century BC, was the beginning of what is now known as the Pre-Socratic period.

During this period, thinkers like Thales, Anaximander, Heraclitus, and Parmenides pondered over the fundamental nature of the universe. They sought to understand the underlying principles of existence, eschewing mythological interpretations in favor of logical reasoning and empirical observation.

The Great Philosophers: Socrates, Plato, and Aristotle

The philosophical journey in Greece is invariably marked by the contributions of three pivotal figures: Socrates, Plato, and Aristotle. Their teachings, which emerged during the Classical period, have transcended centuries, persisting in the heart of Greek culture and, more broadly, the world.

Socrates, often considered the father of Western philosophy, was a quintessential Athenian. Known for his Socratic method – a form of dialogue-based inquiry designed to stimulate critical thinking – he was a champion of intellectual exploration. Despite not having any written records of his own, his teachings were widely documented by his students, most notably Plato.

Plato, a student of Socrates, was a philosopher and mathematician of remarkable depth and breadth. He founded the Academy in Athens, the Western world's first institution of higher learning. His dialogues, which explore topics like justice, beauty, equality, and political governance, have shaped philosophical thought for millennia.

Aristotle, a student of Plato, was a polymath whose interests spanned numerous fields. His empirical approach to studying nature, his development of deductive reasoning, and his views on ethics and aesthetics have left an indelible mark on Western thought.

The Hellenistic Period and Beyond

The Hellenistic period, following the death of Aristotle, saw the rise of several philosophical schools, including Stoicism, Epicureanism, and Skepticism. The Stoics, such as Zeno and Epictetus, advocated for self-control and fortitude as a means to overcome destructive emotions. Epicurus, the founder of Epicureanism, promoted a lifestyle in pursuit of pleasure, particularly those that bring long-term satisfaction and peace. Skeptics, as their name suggests, promoted questioning and doubted the possibility of absolute knowledge.

Greek Philosophy Today

Today, Greek philosophy continues to resonate in every corner of the globe. Its influence is felt in diverse fields such as politics, medicine, metaphysics, ethics, and psychology. Its fundamental questions – What is the nature of reality? What is the good life? What is knowledge? – continue to inspire and provoke thought.

In Greece, the legacy of its philosophical heritage is everywhere. The Academy of Athens, the modern successor of Plato's school, continues to promote learning and research. Philosophy-themed tours offer visitors a unique opportunity to engage with Greek philosophical heritage in a meaningful way.

So, as you walk the streets of Athens, visit the ruins of ancient schools, or gaze at the Mediterranean Sea, let the spirit of Greek philosophy inspire you. Let it engage your intellect, stir your curiosity, and give you a fresh perspective on life. Greek philosophy, after all, is more than just an intellectual tradition; it is a testament to humanity's unending quest for wisdom and understanding.

SOCRATES

CHAPTER 21: DECIPHERING ANCIENT GREEK ART

A *rt is the mirror of a civilization, reflecting its ideals, values, and worldview. In Greece, a country steeped in history and culture, art is more than just an aesthetic pursuit. It is a celebration of the human spirit, a testament to the creative genius that has characterized this nation for millennia. Embarking on a voyage through the mesmerizing realm of Greek art, we will delve into its profound depths, discovering its inception, its evolution, and the indelible impact it has left on the world. Along this journey, we will travel from the ancient pottery adorned with meticulous geometric patterns to the stunningly lifelike statues of the classical era, all the while revealing the rich narratives that these artistic creations embody. This exploration, designed for both the seasoned art connoisseur and the casual observer, promises an enthralling amalgamation of visual delight and intellectual enrichment. We invite you to immerse yourself in the aesthetic grandeur of Greek art, and to appreciate the historical and cultural contexts that gave rise to such extraordinary works of human creativity.*

THE DAWN OF GREEK ART: THE GEOMETRIC PERIOD

Our journey begins in the Geometric period (900-700 BC), a time when Greek art was defined by its simple, geometric patterns. The art of this period, primarily seen on pottery, tells us a great deal about the society that produced it. Funeral scenes, for instance, hint at the Greeks' deep-rooted customs and beliefs in the afterlife.

The Emergence of Realism: The Archaic Period

The Archaic period (700-480 BC) brought substantial changes in Greek art. Sculpture became increasingly significant, with artists creating 'Kouros' and 'Kore' - free-standing male and female statues. These statues, although formal in posture, show an evolving sense of naturalism and the human form.

The Pinnacle of Artistic Excellence: The Classical Period

The Classical period (480-323 BC) is often considered the pinnacle of Greek art. This period is characterized by a heightened sense of realism, balance, and harmony. The iconic Parthenon on the Acropolis, with its Doric columns and frieze depicting the Panathenaic procession, is a prime example of the architectural achievements of this era. Furthermore, the sculptures of this period, crafted by masters like Phidias, Myron, and Polyclitus, are renowned for their idealized human forms that emphasize grace, beauty, and strength.

Art for the Masses: The Hellenistic Period

The The Hellenistic period (323-31 BC) marked a transformative era in Greek art that began following the death of Alexander the Great. This period was characterized by a dynamic shift in artistic style and thematic focus, leading to the creation of art that was more expressive, dramatic, and emotionally charged than ever before.

Artists during the Hellenistic period sought to capture the full spectrum of human experience in their works, focusing on emotions, individuality, and realistic portrayals of everyday life. This was a significant departure from the idealized representations of the Classical period, as Hellenistic artists aimed to depict the world as they saw it, with all its beauty, complexity, and inherent contradictions.

Portraits became deeply personal, reflecting the unique character and emotions of the subject. Sculptures showcased a wide range of human forms and emotions, from the powerful dynamism of the Laocoön Group to the poignant tenderness of the Sleeping Eros. Even the gods, traditionally depicted as paragons of perfection, were portrayed in more human-like forms, revealing their vulnerabilities and passions.

The Hellenistic period also marked a time of geographic expansion for Greek art, propelled by the far-reaching conquests of Alexander the Great. As Greek influence spread across diverse regions from Egypt to India, so too did its artistic traditions. This led to a fascinating cross-pollination of artistic styles, as Greek artists incorporated foreign elements into their work and local artists in the conquered territories adopted Greek techniques and motifs. The result was a period of artistic production that was as diverse as it was innovative, leaving a lasting legacy that continues to inspire and captivate art lovers to this day. It was during the Hellenistic period that Greek art truly became a world art, touching the farthest corners of the known world with its aesthetic brilliance and emotional depth.

Greek Art Today: An Enduring Legacy

Today, Greek art continues to fascinate and inspire. Its influence can be seen in various art movements throughout history and in the modern works of artists worldwide. In Greece, the legacy of its artistic heritage is visible in its numerous museums and archaeological sites.

The National Archaeological Museum in Athens, the Archaeological Museum of Delphi, and the Heraklion Archaeological Museum in Crete house a wealth of Greek artistic treasures. As you walk through these museums, you are not merely observing artifacts; you are traversing the pages of Greek history. Each artifact, each sculpture, and each painting echoes the events, beliefs, and thoughts of the era it belongs to.

Engaging with Greek art is not just about appreciating its aesthetic beauty, but also about understanding the socio-cultural context that gave birth to it. So, as you marvel at the sculptures, mosaics, and pottery, remember that each piece is a window to the past - a testament to Greece's enduring legacy in the world of art.

The journey through Greek art is a journey through time, culture, and the human spirit. It invites us to see the world through the eyes of those who lived millennia ago, to appreciate the beauty they created, and to understand the ideals they upheld. So, as you delve into the world of Greek art, let the works speak to you, let the stories unfold, and let the beauty of this ancient civilization inspire you.

Embracing Greece with Responsibility and Awe

*A*s our journey comes to its conclusion, let us pause to reflect on the importance of traveling responsibly. Greece, with its abundant natural beauty and rich cultural heritage, deserves our utmost respect and mindful presence. Whether it's by supporting local businesses, reducing our plastic usage, respecting wildlife and marine life, or understanding and respecting local customs and traditions, each one of us can contribute positively to the preservation of this mesmerizing land.

Remember, when we travel, we are not just visitors but ambassadors of our own cultures. Let us aim to leave Greece just as beautiful as we found it - or perhaps, even better.

Our guide has taken you through the bustling streets of Athens, the tranquil beaches of its lesser-known islands, the awe-inspiring ancient ruins, the vibrant festivals, and the delectable Greek cuisine. It has revealed the secrets of Greek wine, introduced you to the fascinating world of Greek mythology, and provided essential tips for a memorable and hassle-free travel experience.

But, as the saying goes, 'seeing is believing.' The magic of Greece can only be truly experienced when you're there, feeling the warmth of the sun on your skin, tasting the salt in the air, hearing the rhythmic strumming of a bouzouki, and seeing the world through the lens of its rich and timeless history.

As the Greek philosopher **Socrates** once said, "I am not an Athenian or a Greek, but a citizen of the world." In the spirit of Socrates, let us embark on this journey as citizens of the world, ready to learn, to appreciate, and to immerse ourselves in the extraordinary realm that is Greece. Your journey is about to begin - embrace it, cherish it, and let it inspire you.

As we draw this journey to a close, I am filled with gratitude. To you, dear reader, for sharing this adventure; to the individuals who contributed their stories and wisdom; to my supportive family and friends; and to Greece, our guide and muse, I extend my sincerest thanks. As you embark on your own journey, may you experience the joy and wonder that has imbued this project. In the immortal words of the Greeks, "Καλό ταξίδι" - safe travels.

Your adventure awaits.

Stevan Clark

Made in United States
Troutdale, OR
12/13/2023